Mother Earth, Father Sky

Mother Earth, Father Sky

NATIVE AMERICAN MYTH

MYTH AND MANKIND

MOTHER EARTH, FATHER SKY: Native American Myth
Writers: Tom Lowenstein (The Indian World, Earthdivers
and Creators, Spiritual Cosmos, Keepers of Order)
Piers Vitebsky (A Web of Ceremony, The Native
American Legacy)
Consultants: Hugh Brodie, Alan Marshall

Created, edited and designed by
Duncan Baird Publishers
Castle House
75–76 Wells Street
London W1P 3RE

DUNCAN BAIRD PUBLISHERS
Managing Editor: Stephen Adamson
Managing Art Editor: Gabriella Le Grazie
Editors: Peter Lewis, Margaret Mulvihill, Ruth Petrie
Designers: Gabriella Le Grazie, Christine Keilty
Picture Researcher: Cee Weston-Baker
Artworks: Neil Gower
Map Artworks: Lorraine Harrison
Artwork Borders: Iona McGlashan
Editorial Researcher: Simon Ryder
Editorial Assistant: Andrea Buzyn

TIME-LIFE BOOKS
Staff for MOTHER EARTH, FATHER SKY:
Native American Myth:
Editorial Manager: Tony Allan
Design Consultant: Mary Staples
Editorial Production: Justina Cox

Published by Time-Life Books BV, Amsterdam

First Time-Life English language printing 1997

TIME-LIFE is a trademark of
Time Warner Inc, USA

ISBN 0 7054 3523 7

Colour separation by Colourscan, Singapore
Printed and bound by Milanostampa, SpA, Farigliano, Italy

Cover pictures:
Title page: Mask of a girl, constructed of wood and braided
human hair. Each plait of hair is secured with grips which
open out to reveal a bird with outstretched wings. This
intricate artefact was made by a craftsman of the
Tsimshian people of the Northwest Coast.
Contents page: A wooden mask from the Pacific
Northwest Coast.

Contents

THE INDIAN WORLD

For decades, the Lakota Sioux of South Dakota had fiercely resisted white encroachment on their ancestral homelands, but by the harsh winter of 1890 they were becoming increasingly beleaguered. Three years earlier, the US President had been granted wide-ranging powers to "detribalize" Native Americans, and in 1889 the break-up of the Great Sioux Reservation began. The proud nation that had crushed Custer's Seventh Cavalry at the Battle of Little Big Horn in 1876 was faced with disaster.

In the midst of such depredation, just one desperate hope of salvation remained: in 1889 a Paiute holy man named Wovoka had prophesied the deliverance of the Indians from white domination. The people's dead ancestors would bring this about, so to ensure their resurrection Wovoka had instituted a ceremony known as the Ghost Dance. A revivalist movement based on it found fertile ground among the demoralized Sioux and other nations of the Plains. So zealous were its followers that they even donned special shirts, believing them to be impervious to bullets. The Sioux chief Sitting Bull had been sceptical at first, but later lent his support. Feared by the whites, the veteran leader had thus become the figurehead of a ritual that he never personally took part in.

On December 15 1890, a devastating blow fell on the Sioux. As policemen recruited from among the very people who had once fought alongside Sitting Bull tried to arrest him at Standing Rock Reservation, fighting broke out. At the end of a brief but bloody skirmish, the legendary warrior lay dead. He was buried without ceremony two days later.

With their leader gone, Sitting Bull's followers fled south, joining up with the Ghost Dancers on the Cheyenne River Reservation. But their leader, Big Foot, himself was a wanted man, so the combined group of over 300 people kept heading south through the Badlands. They were intercepted by cavalrymen on December 28 and diverted to Wounded Knee Creek. The next morning, the troops moved in to disarm the Sioux. Suddenly, a shot rang out; a warrior had accidentally fired his weapon. The result was carnage; nervous soldiers shooting point-blank with rifles and cannon slaughtered 250 Lakota.

Not only were the lives of men, women and children extinguished by the terrible massacre. In the words of Black Elk, one of the few survivors: "Something else died in the bloody mud and was buried in the blizzard. A people's dream died there".

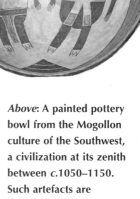

Above: **A painted pottery bowl from the Mogollon culture of the Southwest, a civilization at its zenith between *c*.1050–1150. Such artefacts are evidence of the diverse creativity of Native American societies before the arrival of Europeans.**

Left: **The Brulé Sioux chief He-Dog, photographed in the early 20th century by John Alvin Anderson. The Sioux were among the last Native peoples to resist white domination.**

The First Americans

At the time of the first European contact at the outset of the sixteenth century, as many as 600 distinct nations or tribes were living in North America. Several million indigenous people inhabited the continent, with a variety of ways of life adapted to the varying climate and topography.

Traditionally North America was thought to have been peopled by nomadic hunters, who crossed the Beringia land bridge linking Asia and the Americas during the last Ice Age and spread south over the course of six thousand years. Although some more recent archaeological finds from South America may indicate earlier human occupation, there is as yet no firm evidence of a human presence in North America before around 15,000BC.

The first Americans were all hunter-gatherers, but some herding and farming cultures developed over time. For example, by AD700 the area encompassing much of present-day Arizona, Utah, Colorado and New Mexico had become home to the ancestors of the peoples known now as the Pueblo. They lived in adobe (mud brick) villages near rivers, which fed irrigation canals; these allowed them to cultivate biannual crops of corn, as well as plentiful beans, squash and cotton. At around the same time, communities living in Mississippian river valleys built the first true North American towns. The most widely studied of these pre-Columbian "mound cultures", Cahokia, was inhabited at its zenith by at least 10,000 people. But these sites were abandoned before the first European contact, probably in about AD1450, as a result of epidemic diseases.

The Impact of Europeans

The first Europeans to arrive in North America settled near the coasts and navigable rivers, but later began to move deep into the wooded hinterland in search of furs and new farming land. They also wished to consolidate their political and religious authority in this uncharted country. The territorial

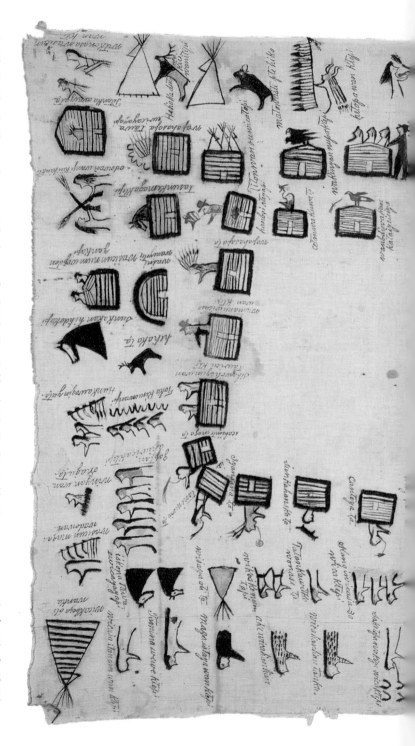

A Dakota Sioux "Winter Count" (c.1890), a detailed calendar of events painted on a buffalo hide. This late example of a traditional method of recording history is indicative of the highly developed social structures that existed in Native American communities prior to the arrival of Europeans.

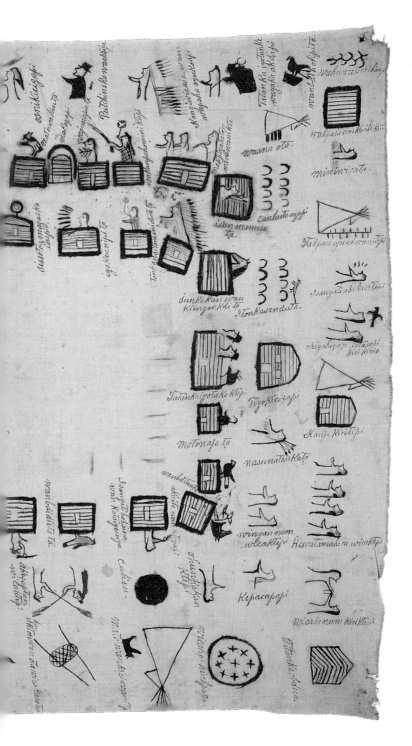

ambitions of the white settlers – whose acquisitiveness was at variance with the Native American attitude to the natural world – soon brought them into conflict with indigenous peoples. Although political and commercial alliances that were expedient for both parties were formed, they were ultimately to cause the displacement of many settled peoples. For instance, the fur trade was lucrative to both whites and some Indians, but it created great upheaval for other Natives. In its early days, this trade was dominated by five Iroquois groups (the Cayuga, Mohawk, Oneida, Onondaga and Seneca), who were armed by Dutch and English settlers. These groups drove the Ojibway southwards from Lake Superior, and they, in turn, pushed the Sioux on to the Plains. As punishment for their alliance with the British, the Iroquois themselves were later displaced during the American War of Independence (1775–83).

Growing European incursion into the North American interior during the nineteenth century saw Native peoples driven relentlessly westwards. The Indian Removal Act, passed by the US Congress in 1830, forcibly removed five tribes from their original homelands in the southeast and resettled them west of the Mississippi. The Act provided for a new enclave of "Indian Territory" in an area covering the modern states of Kansas and Oklahoma, as well as parts of Nebraska, Colorado and Wyoming, but even this fell victim to white encroachment after mineral wealth was discovered in the region. Just one example of genocide at this time was the brutal expulsion of Native peoples inhabiting areas affected by the gold rushes of the late 1840s onwards. The populous Shoshoni, Ute and Paiute of northern California and Nevada were swiftly extirpated.

Prior to the arrival of Europeans, the lives of many Native North Americans had revolved around seasonal hunting activities. This was especially true of the cultures that inhabited the vast plains in the middle of the continent. Here, big-game hunting was generally a male preserve, while women were responsible for gathering and gardening. For centuries, Plains Indians had stalked the buffalo on foot. Initially, white influence brought prosperity by making hunting easier; horses were taken from Spanish settlers, who did not allow Indians to own them, in the seventeenth century. By the mid-1700s, the horse, known to Native peoples as "Spirit Dog" or "Medicine Dog", was allowing Cheyenne, Osage, Sioux and Pawnee buffalo-hunters to range across vast areas.

However, as the nineteenth century progressed, white frontiersmen systematically exterminated the buffalo population – for their meat and hides and to protect new railway development – and so eroded the basis of Plains culture. In one three-year period alone (1872–74), some 3 million animals were killed. By the 1880s, from a population that once totalled 90 million, only 1000 buffalo remained, two-thirds of them in Canada.

In concert with the eradication of the animals on which their livelihood depended, the Plains peoples faced a sustained onslaught on their cultural traditions and religious observances. Many rites were outlawed because reformers saw them as obstacles to the assimilation of Native Americans into white culture ("Americanization"). Most notable of these was the Sun Dance, an eight-day-long ceremony of thanksgiving to the Great Spirit and the buffalo, which was outlawed by the US government in 1884. The Bureau of Indian Affairs also promoted policies that prohibited the use of Native languages. In 1887, Congress passed the Dawes Act, which broke up tribal lands into European-style homesteading lots of 160 acres. In addition, schools were established to inculcate Christian values in Native Americans, principal among which was the "love of personal property". It was in this atmosphere of complete white dominance that the Ghost Dance evolved, as a despairing attempt to affirm a dying culture.

This hand drum belonged to a shaman of the Assiniboine people of the northern Plains. The Assiniboine were just one of the nations of this vast region to suffer greatly from white incursion in the 19th century. A smallpox epidemic carried by traders in 1837 severely reduced their numbers, while buffalo hunting wiped out the animal on which their livelihood depended.

Passing on Sacred Wisdom

Knowledge of the diverse spirit forces that were believed to pervade the physical world was essential to Native Americans. Spiritual wisdom was conveyed in the form of myths and legends narrated by storytellers or community elders.

For Native audiences, myths were far from being fantastic "fairytales" even when, as was common, they involved magical phenomena, such as animals talking to one another or people conversing with animals and spirits. Rather, stories were seen as accounts of real events that took place at the dawn of time.

The purpose of myths and legends was both to instruct and to entertain. For instance, a familiar character from stories of many cultures was the clownish Trickster. This ambiguous figure was both sacred and profane, and his antics were intended to provoke thought and laughter in equal measure.

Storytelling occupied a seminal position in Native American cultures. It was not a purely spoken art: singing and drumming were often involved.

Moreover, details from myths were often depicted on artefacts in daily use. Pottery, baskets, blankets, storage boxes and robes were decorated with patterns or symbols that had their origin in narratives.

One of the most highly developed artistic traditions was among the societies of the Northwest Coast, whose masks and totem poles portrayed numerous characters from mythology and history. In the same way, the kachina figures created by the southwestern Hopi people represent an extensive range of mythical and ancestral spirits.

A kachina doll from the Hopi of the Southwest. Kachinas are spirits that embody human qualities or natural phenomena, and are the subject of many of this culture's myths.

The Native American Revival

After the massacre at Wounded Knee, Native American communities were in a parlous state. Confined to reservations and divorced from their traditional ways of life, their existence was blighted by poverty and sickness. Their hardship was ignored by white Americans who, once the Indian "threat" had receded, trivialized their culture, treating it as merely an exotic footnote to frontier history. "Buffalo Bill" Cody's sham "Wild West" pageants, which began even as real Plains culture was being destroyed in the 1880s, remained popular until well into the twentieth century.

Official policy tacitly assumed that Native peoples would become extinct, and so no strategy was devised regarding their future. However, from the 1930s onwards (notably the Indian Reorganization Act), attempts were made to reverse hostile land reform and restore tribal integrity. Native populations began slowly to increase after decades of decline, and many communities elected to adopt written constitutions. The resilience of Native North Americans owes much to their spiritual heritage – and especially the bond between people and nature that forms the bedrock of Indian culture.

A Tapestry of Peoples

North America is a vast and varied continent containing extremes of climate and topography. Its environments range from the frozen wastes of the Arctic to the tropical swamps of the Southeast. Native tribes are normally grouped according to the regions they inhabit.

The Northeast

The woodlands, lakes and rivers of the Northeast, where the first British, French and Dutch traders and settlers were active, were inhabited by Algonquian and Iroquoian-speaking peoples. They fished the rivers and lakes from birch-bark canoes, and hunted and gathered food in the forest. The Iroquoian people also cultivated parts of their territory as fields for corn (maize), beans and squash.

The Algonquian-speakers lived in wigwams – domed homes made of tree bark – or less permanent tipis made of animal hides. Algonquian society was highly egalitarian, with no hierarchical structure. The economy was based on a mix of hunting and the gathering of wild plant species.

The area around the eastern Great Lakes was inhabited by the Iroquoian-speakers, who lived in stockaded villages of longhouses, built of wood and sited around communal gardens. Senior

Right: **Map of the Native American cultural regions, showing the location of the main peoples.**

Below: **Fishing provided an important supply of food to people of the Northeast, the Plateau and the Northwest. This early 20th-century photograph shows Spokane Indians fishing from a canoe on the Pend Oreille River in Washington State.**

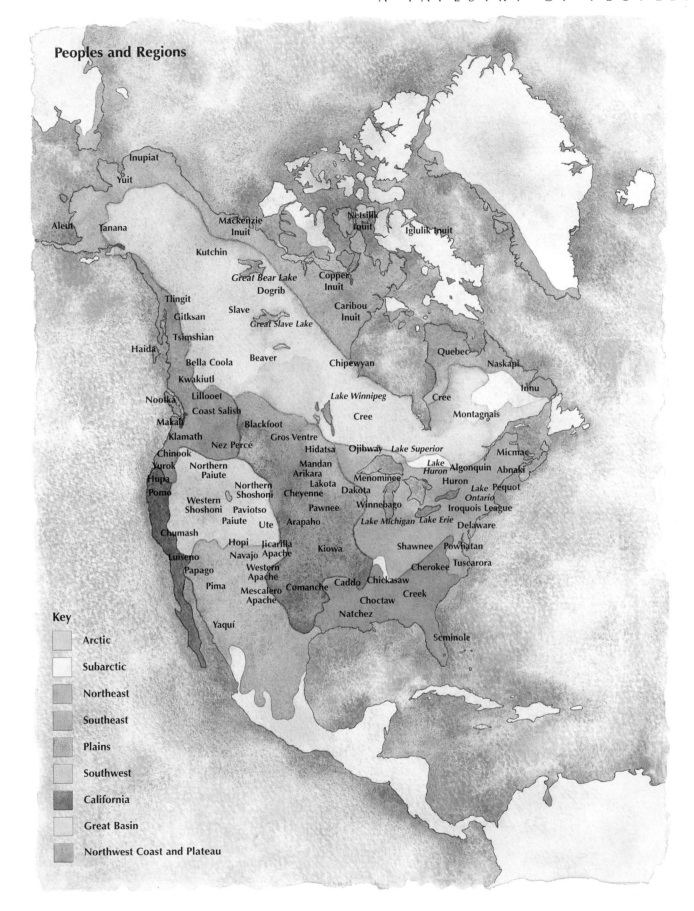

Peoples and Regions

Inupiat
Yuit
Aleut
Tanana
Mackenzie Inuit
Netsilik Inuit
Iglulik Inuit
Kutchin
Great Bear Lake
Copper Inuit
Dogrib
Caribou Inuit
Tlingit
Slave
Gitksan
Great Slave Lake
Tsimshian
Haida
Beaver
Bella Coola
Chipewyan
Quebec
Naskapi
Kwakiutl
Innu
Nootka
Lilooet
Cree
Makah
Coast Salish
Lake Winnipeg
Cree
Montagnais
Klamath
Blackfoot
Gros Ventre
Nez Percé
Micmac
Chinook
Hidatsa
Ojibway
Lake Superior
Yurok
Mandan
Lake Huron
Algonquin
Abnaki
Northern Paiute
Arikara
Menominee
Huron
Hupa
Northern Shoshoni
Lakota
Cheyenne
Dakota
Lake Ontario
Pequot
Pomo
Western Shoshoni
Paviotso
Pawnee
Winnebago
Iroquois League
Paiute
Ute
Arapaho
Lake Michigan
Lake Erie
Delaware
Chumash
Hopi
Jicarilla Apache
Kiowa
Shawnee
Powhatan
Luiseno
Navajo
Tuscarora
Papago
Western Apache
Cherokee
Pima
Mescalero Apache
Comanche
Caddo
Chickasaw
Creek
Choctaw
Yaquí
Natchez
Seminole

Key

- Arctic
- Subarctic
- Northeast
- Southeast
- Plains
- Southwest
- California
- Great Basin
- Northwest Coast and Plateau

13

men acted as the chiefs of these communities, while older women were responsible for tending the gardens and the tribe's cornfields. Despite being initially fewer in number than the Algonquian peoples surrounding them, the Iroquoians came to dominate the Northeast by the end of the seventeenth century.

The Southeast

The tribes living in southeastern America, the area ranging from the Appalachian Mountains to Florida and the Gulf of Mexico, and west of the Mississippi to Texas, enjoyed a mainly lush and fertile country. The peoples of this region inhabited villages; typical dwellings, such as those of the Creek, comprised rectangular, mud-plastered summer houses and conical winter houses set partly in the ground to aid insulation. The culture of the southeastern peoples bears traces of the prehistoric Mississippian civilization. The Chickasaw, Cherokee, Creek, Choctaw and Seminoles were described as "The Five Civilized Tribes" by Europeans, because of their affluence

and adaptability, and Cherokee was the first Native American language for which a written form was devised, in the 1820s. However, accommodation with whites did not prevent their being forcibly displaced westwards in 1830 (see page 9), a journey known to the Cherokee as "the Trail of Tears". Their myths and legends continue to affirm their bonds with their ancient southeastern homelands.

The Plains

Between the Mississippi River and the Rocky Mountains are the grasslands known as the Plains, or prairies (now largely given over to the cultivation of cereals). Over the last millennium, the Plains have been the home of many tribes, some of whom were more or less permanently nomadic buffalo hunters, while others alternated between hunting on the Plains and living in more settled villages in adjacent forested areas.

The introduction of the horse had a huge impact on Plains life. Some people who had adopted a settled crop-growing existence, living in

TIMELINE Native American History	c.50,000–10,000BC	10,000–7000BC	7000–1500BC	1500BC–AD1000
Before c.15,000BC, the Americas began to be peopled by Asian nomadic hunters who crossed the land bridge that stretched across the Bering Straits. Humans had established themselves throughout the Americas by 8000BC; the first signs of a settled society are the so-called Woodland cultures of the east, in c.1400BC.	15,000BC Earliest evidence of human life in North America. 13,000–11,000BC Glacial resurgence leads to extensive migration southwards. 10,000BC Climatic warming; development of archaic human cultures of generalized hunter-gatherers.	10,000–8000BC Last Ice Age (Pleistocene) ends. c.9000BC Mammoths and other large Ice Age game animals begin to become extinct. Desert culture established in Great Basin. c.7000BC Cultivation of many species of wild plant begins (e.g. squash, pumpkins, gourds, beans and peppers).		

These Sandia spear points are from a Southwest desert culture dated around 10,000BC.

A pueblo of the Anasazi culture of the Southwest

Formative Period of Native North American culture. 5000–3500BC Cultivated strain of maize introduced. 2500–1500BC Animals domesticated in villages; pottery and weaving.

1400BC Growth of Eastern mound cultures (Adena, Hopewell, Mississippian). c.300BC Rise of Mogollon culture in the Southwest. c.100BC Hohokam and Anasazi cultures develop in the Southwest. c.AD750 Pueblo period; adobe villages first built.

earth and grass houses, abandoned them for the tipi, whose poles and buffalo-hide covers were easily transported on horses. Some of the tribes most strongly associated with buffalo hunting in the nineteenth century moved to the Plains only at a relatively late stage. The Cheyenne, for example, whose ancestral homelands were near the Great Lakes, had moved to the Plains in the early nineteenth century and became year-round buffalo hunters. Although the Plains became the scene of fierce rivalry between competing tribes, its peoples shared a sign language and a profound belief in a supreme creator, the "Great Spirit".

The Southwest

Two main groups of peoples occupy the plains and canyons of the Southwest. The first, the Hopi, Zuni and Pima, have a rich religious and cultural heritage that harks back to the civilization of the prehistoric Anasazi and Hohokam peoples. They are collectively known as Pueblo peoples, from their villages (Spanish: *pueblos*), which consist of a network of mud-brick (adobe) houses, with

underground chambers used for religious ceremonies. The Pueblo peoples were both farmers and hunter-gatherers, and were – and still are – remarkable craftsmen.

Around AD300 this group was joined by another, consisting of two nomadic, Athabascan-speaking peoples, the Navajo and the Apache. Both adopted many aspects of Pueblo culture. For example, the Jicarilla Apache of northern New Mexico learned agriculture from the Pueblos.

California

The boundaries of Native California correspond to those of the modern US state. The sea sustained, among others, the Chumash and Pomo, who traded extensively with Yuma hunter-gatherers inland. From the mid-eighteenth century onwards, the Californian peoples' seasonal routines were disrupted by the activities of Spanish Christian missions on the coast. Gradually, the tribes were divested of their language and religious traditions. Then the gold rush of 1848–49 brought widespread disease and dispossession to the region.

AD1000–1600	17th century	18th century	19th century	20th century

AD1050–1150 Height of Mississippian culture.
***c.*1275** Many Pueblo settlements abandoned.
1497 Eastern seaboard of North America explored by Europeans.
1513 Spanish expeditions encroach on the Southeast from Mexico.

This copper warrior's profile, made c.1200, was found in Oklahoma.

Use of the horse begins among Native Americans; increasing contact with Europeans brings devastating diseases.
1607 English colonists establish Jamestown, their first permanent settlement.
1622 Jamestown attacked by Powhatan Confederacy.
1695 Pima uprising against the Spanish in the Southwest.
1697 First of many colonial wars between European powers; the French and their Algonquian allies fight the British.

Wholesale displacement, genocide and enslavement of Indians by whites.
1763–64 Pontiac's Rebellion against British in Great Lakes area. First major Indian insurrection.
1776 US Independence followed by further acts of dispossession.
1776–87 First Indian reservations in Northeast. Forced removals continue despite treaties enshrining Indian land rights.
1799 Seneca chief Handsome Lake founds the Longhouse religion, first Indian revivalist movement.

1830 Indian Removal Act forces Natives to relocate west to "Indian Territory".
1865–85 Plains buffalo herds slaughtered.
1876 Sioux/Cheyenne alliance defeats US Cavalry under Custer.
1890 Indian Wars end with massacre of Sioux at Wounded Knee.

Pueblo Indians pose with the US flag in the 1920s.

1918 Native American Church founded.
1934 US Government provides for tribal self-government.
1968 American Indian Movement (AIM) founded.

The Great Basin

The Great Basin, the ancient dry lake-beds between the Rockies and the Sierra Nevada, was home to the Ute, Paiute and Shoshoni. Prior to white encroachment, these peoples lived by hunting and fishing; later, as they were forced to subsist on roots and seeds, they became known as "Digger Indians". They also trapped reptiles and small mammals. Lean-to structures or (especially in prehistoric times) semi-subterranean homes were their commonest form of dwelling. The California Gold Rush of 1848–49 triggered a white invasion of the region, which was annexed by the US government in 1864. Following this, the original inhabitants were decimated by disease and then confined within reservations.

A Haida woman from the Northwest Coast painting a woven reed hat, photographed in about 1900.

The Northwest Coast

From northern California to southeast Alaska, the North American coast is home to numerous cultures. This is a prosperous region: the sea and rivers teem with fish and sea mammals, while the thick forests yield an abundance of game and berries. Northwest Coast societies are renowned for their rich artistic tradition and complex social structures. Some peoples, such as the Haida, were even slave-owning, whom they captured on maritime raids.

Most peoples of the region were divided into clans, each of which had its particular crest, such as the Killer Whale, Wolf, Raven and Frog. These were carved or painted on the cedarwood houses and "totem poles" that strongly characterize the region. Another distinctive feature of Northwest Coast life was the potlatch, a public ceremony in which clans asserted their property rights and prestige by giving away or destroying possessions.

The Plateau

Inland from the Northwest Coast is the Plateau region, which is crossed by a number of major rivers. These supply the villages of various peoples, including the Nez Percé (French: "pierced nose"), Cayuse and Lillooet, with many species of fish. The Plateau people are noted for their skills as both hunters and gatherers. After the Nez Percé and the Shoshoni acquired horses in the late seventeenth century, they became seasonal buffalo hunters on the western Plains.

The Subarctic

North of the Plains and the Great Lakes lie the cold rivers and dense forests of the Subarctic. Its Native inhabitants comprised Athabascan-speakers, such as the Dogrib, Chipewyan, Slave, Koyukon and Kutchin, and Algonquian speakers, such as the Cree and Ojibway. These nomads lived in small groups that varied

Native American Languages

The Siberian nomads who first peopled the Americas are thought to have brought with them several ancient languages, all evidence of which has been lost. These developed into a huge range of tongues – perhaps as many as 2200. Although many of these became extinct under white domination, it is estimated that Native American peoples north of Mexico still speak about 300 languages, within which there are some 2000 distinct dialects.

This modern Sioux painting (1951) by the Dakota artist Oscar Howe shows a tribal elder teaching. Until recently, most Native American languages were unwritten, so wisdom and instruction were traditionally passed on by word of mouth.

Owing to extensive migration within the North American continent, languages belonging to the same family often have a wide geographical distribution. Eskimo-Aleut tongues, for instance, are spoken throughout the length and breadth of the Arctic. More surprisingly, the Apache and the Navajo of the Southwest speak languages of the Athabascan family, whose other speakers (e.g. the Dogrib of Northwest Territory) live far away in the western Subarctic.

Indian precontact writing was in the form of pictographs – literal representations of objects and events. The only true Indian phonetic script is that devised by

the Cherokee Sequoyah in the early nineteenth century.

Many indigenous people still speak a Native language. There

are at least 100,000 speakers of Navajo, while the Gros Ventre of Montana have revived their once-extinct language.

their way of life according to the season. In winter they hunted large game, but turned to fishing in spring. The southern forests yielded berries and wildfowl, as well as porcupines, whose quills were used to ornament clothing. In the 1700s, Subarctic peoples changed from hunting and gathering to a more diverse economy based on trading fur pelts with whites.

The Arctic

The Arctic, a vast frozen territory, encompasses Siberia, Alaska, northern Canada and Greenland. People began to hunt and fish along its coasts around 5000 years ago. These first inhabitants,

known to anthropologists as the Dorset people, were displaced or absorbed by the Inuit, or Eskimo, who arrived from Asia in around AD1000–1200. Inuit simply means "people", while "Eskimo" derives from an old Algonquian word for "meat eaters". The Inuit either lead a semi-nomadic existence, moving between the coast and inland areas, or live a more settled life in coastal villages, reliant on whale and walrus hunting. While the Canadian Inuit have traditionally built temporary snow houses (igloos) on the frozen sea, Alaskan Inuit winter in semi-underground earth-houses. Inuktitut, the language of the Inuit, has two dialect groups, and there is a wide range of mutual intelligibility across the Arctic.

SACRED PLACES

Native Americans hold all features of the natural environment in reverence. Yet some places are thought to possess more sacred power than others. Imposing mountains and cliffs, and sites near water are regarded as particularly pregnant with spiritual force. Yet this power can even inhabit individual trees and rocks. Some places are hallowed in myth either for their supernatural origin or as the location of important events. Whatever their particular significance, all sacred places help affirm peoples' sense of identity, and are thus favoured sites for ceremonies of thanks and propitiation, or for vision quests, initiation rites and burials. All Native Americans treat their locality with great respect, lest the spirit forces living there take umbrage and do them harm.

Above: Between AD850 and 1150, Cahokia in Missouri was a major spiritual site, with over 100 pyramids, temples and burial mounds.

Dramatic peaks such as Big Foot Pass (left) in the Badlands of South Dakota and striking mountain formations or buttes, such as Church Rock in Utah (top), could hold sacred and mythological meanings or be used by shamans for their vision quests. The Canyon de Chelly, Arizona (above left) was a sacred site, in turn, for the Anasazi, Hopi and Navajo.

According to the myths of the Northwest Coast peoples, the mountain of Stek-ya-den in British Columbia (above) was a place of retribution and death. Spirit-animal petroglyphs (right) are found at Crooked River in Oregon. Often located on dramatic rock formations, petroglyph sites were used for ceremonial purposes.

EARTHDIVERS AND CREATORS

Prairie Falcon and Crow were sitting on a log that rose from the waters covering the world. It was the beginning of time. There was no land; no people as we know them. But playing on the primal waters were other birds: Duck, Coot and Grebe. And though Falcon and Crow were powerful fliers, that was not the skill that was required for the task ahead, which was to finish creating the world. Somewhere in the depths, Falcon and Crow prophetically surmised, was earth. Only a great diver willing to risk the enormous journey could succeed in fetching it up.

Duck dived, entered a mystical dream and died. Coot followed, but he also failed. Finally Grebe descended. He reached the bottom, grabbed some sand in each hand and floated, lifeless now, back to the surface. All three birds were revived by the magical powers of Falcon. When Grebe returned to life, no-one believed that he'd touched the bottom. "Look under my nails," answered Grebe to their mocking laughter. Sure enough, the sand was there. So the birds took the sand and threw it in every direction across the water. And that, according to an old story of the Californian Mono people, is how birds made the world.

This origin story is a classic example of an "earthdiver" myth in which the world rose from the primal waters with the magical help of birds or animals. Other stories tell how people emerged from a gloomy underworld. These primal days are seen as a time when people and animals shared thoughts and language; when vast, often vague, creative powers could achieve anything; when creators like Raven, Coyote or Old Man walked the earth and made natural features, animals and people as they are today.

There are innumerable Native American creation myths. But common to most of them is the sense that human beings were created as the companions, not the masters, of all other creatures. In the mythical time of the Native American imagination, people, animals, all things that grow, and the rocks and earth of the world itself are created equal. And among all the people that know of this mythical time this equality is cherished.

Above: Among the Sierra Nevada Mountains by the German artist Albert Bierstadt (1830–1902). This landscape was sacred for the local Maidu people.

Left: The face of Nass-Shaki-Yeil, creator god of the Northwest Coast. He was the hoarder of light and the grandfather of the Trickster Raven. This frontlet was made *c.*1850 by a Tsimshian craftsman.

21

Earthdivers

A duck, a grebe, a beetle or a crayfish: these were the intrepid divers of early creation. They plunged into the murky depths of Earth's primal waters to bring up grains of sand or mud, which then grew vast and became the terrestrial world.

Up in the sky, before the world was made, people lived in a village at whose centre grew a tree with huge white flowers. These blossoms gave light to the people in the sky, and when they fell, the sky grew darker. In the course of time a woman had a dream. In it she received a message: "The tree must be uprooted!" After some discussion in the village, the sky folk agreed to pull the tree up, but as they did so, the tree sank and disappeared. Angrily, the chief called the woman into his presence, and, as she approached the hole left by the tree, the chief pushed her through it.

The woman fell and fell and, as she looked down, she saw the lower world, the world as we know it. But the form of the lower world had not been finished. The earth was not made. All she could see was water. Swimming on the water and flying above it were enormous numbers of birds. As the woman continued to plummet through the sky towards the water, a duck raised its head.

"How shall we make a resting place for this falling being?" cried the duck. And one after another, the birds began diving to see if the water had a bottom. Eventually the hell-diver bird went deep enough and brought up some earth.

The chief of the birds said: "Put the earth on the turtle's back!" So the beaver pounded the earth on to the turtle's back, and when the woman arrived through the air, they laid her on it. Here, mysteriously, she gave birth, and from her children came all human beings.

This Seneca story from New York State describes the creation of the world in ways characteristic of many Native Americans myths. First, at the beginning of time, there are the "sky people". These are neither real people, nor spirits, nor gods. The sky folk are vague beings, ancestors of that "first mother" who falls to the lower world, and are similar to the later people on Earth. Next, the lower world itself is a vast mass of water, populated by birds and animals. As in most stories from Native American hunting societies, these creatures can think and speak. Typical, too, is the animals' desire to complete the world, which is still only partially created.

In this Seneca story, as in the Mono story (see page 21), a diving bird achieves the task. Sounding the depths of the primal waters, the diver brings up earth which is then plastered on the back of the turtle. And the whole world is thus understood to be an island resting on the back of that original turtle, and surrounded by the original waters.

In some Native American earthdiver stories there is competition between the diving birds and the animals. The strongest and most skilful divers, such as the loon (Great Northern Diver) or the duck, often win the day, but in other tales it is a small and insignificant animal who succeeds. Among the midwestern Cherokee, the victorious earthdiver is a water beetle; while the diver in the creation story of another midwestern people, the Chickasaw, is a crayfish. In these myths, existence

This 19th-century beaded, buckskin purse is in the form of a turtle, the Earth-holding animal of many Native origin stories. Turtles have female associations and this one probably contained a girl baby's umbilical cord. From the cradle to the grave such purses served as protective charms or amulets.

This 19th-century Tlingit shaman's rattle takes the form of a grebe with two smaller birds resting on its back. Grebes and other waterbirds are often cast as the heroes of earthdiver creation stories. They dive into the primal waters to bring up the first fragments of earth, the *terra firma* that makes the creation of people possible.

begins with animals who are at home in water and air. The first project for these creatures is the creation of the earth so that terrestrial beings, humans, can join them in a new world. As soon as there is dry land, there are people to walk upon it.

Native American stories explaining creation usually account only for the territory known by the particular society that owns the myth. Indeed, sometimes creation myths narrate only the origin of limited, albeit significant, parts of a tribal homeland. In northwest Alaska, for example, there is a thin, sandy peninsula called Tikigaq, which projects forty kilometres into the Arctic Ocean. This low-lying and fragile-looking land was slowly formed before the last Ice Age out of sandstone deposits from local sea-cliffs. The Tikigaq Inuit, who have inhabited the peninsula for more than a thousand years, have a story about the origin of their ancestral homeland that accounts for its geological structure.

According to this myth, the existing but incomplete world was inhabited by people and by beings who were half human and half animal. One of these beings was Tulungigraq ("someone like a raven"), a magically created man with the head of a raven (*tulugaq*, "raven"). Tulungigraq's creation work consisted of two main tasks. He was to bring alternating periods of night and day to a world still plunged in darkness, but before doing that he had

to hunt down a whale-like beast that lived in the dark primal waters off the yet unformed Alaska. So Tulungigraq set out with his harpoon and travelled by kayak until he heard the great beast breathing through the night. Singing magical songs, the Raven Man came alongside the animal and harpooned it. The sea beast sank, and as Tulungigraq secured it with his harpoon line, the animal rose again and transformed into land. This new stretch of earth became Tikigaq *nuna* (land): the peninsula which has since been the home of the Tikigaq people.

Like the Seneca earthdiver story, this Tikigaq tale explains how the Earth arose from the primal depths, but this time the agent of creation is a bird-man. These mythical agents of creation work their own magic. No mention is made of a supreme, omnipotent creator.

Raven, the Trickster hero of Northwest Coast creation myths, who brought daylight and fire to the world, forms the handle of this 19th-century Tlingit ladle. Like other birds and the sea animals, Raven was generally thought to have existed before the first people. Made of horn, bone, copper and abalone shell, the ladle may have been used in ceremonies.

23

Of Seasons, Seals and Cereals

The huge variety of natural phenomena, the four elements, and the rhythms of the days and the changing seasons provide themes for a wealth of origin stories. In some myths creation is a side-effect, arising from a conflict between animals; in others, trickster animals such as the keen-eyed Raven of the Inuit, or the subversive Coyote of the Comanches, come to the aid of struggling primordial humans.

Throughout Native American myth, large-scale phenomena, such as day and night, the seasons, water, buffalo and whales, frequently emerge from something tiny and inconsequential. Not only that, but in the process of creating the larger phenomena, the tiny creators themselves sometimes change. One Iroquois tale explains how Chipmunk and Bear quarrelled over the question of daylight. Chipmunk, wanting day and night to alternate, sang: "The light must come. We must have light!" Bear, on the other hand, sang: "Night is best. We must have darkness!" When day began to dawn in

response to Chipmunk's song, Bear was angry and chased his rival up into a tree. His paw grazed Chipmunk's back, leaving an imprint, the two black stripes which stand out on the chipmunk's fur to this day. But he had escaped and his wish that night and day should follow one other had prevailed for all time.

A story of the Northwest Coast Tahltan people describes a quarrel between two other animals, Porcupine and Beaver, over the length of the seasons. To indicate the numbers of winter months he wanted, Porcupine held up five claws. But Beaver held up his tail and said: "Let there be many winter months like the many scratches on my tail!" Angry at being contradicted, Porcupine bit off his own thumb and holding up his hand, cried: "Let it be four months!" Beaver gave in, and since that time the winter in that region has lasted four months, and porcupines have four claws on each foot.

In many Native American stories animals simply exist from the beginning of time. But among the central Inuit of Arctic Canada sea mammals, such as the seal, walrus and whale, were created from the dismembered finger joints of the mythical woman Nuliayuk, who was to become the major sea deity (see page 55).

A story from the Comanche people of the Plains explains how the great herds of buffalo came into being. Back in myth time, all the buffalo were owned by an old woman and a little boy. The animals were kept penned up in the mountains and none of the people could reach them. Trickster Coyote, an animal credited with

This snuff box from western Alaska mimics two seals. The first seals were believed to have been formed from the fingers of the sea deity, Nuliayuk. Men smoked tobacco but women chewed it or took it as snuff.

many mythical interventions (see page 43), held a council with the Indians, and together they decided to send a tiny animal into the buffalo keepers' hideout. The boy, they reasoned, would adopt the animal, and the animal would in turn help release the buffalo. Twice the plan failed; but the third time, despite the old woman's objections, the child managed to hold on to his new pet. That night the creature escaped from him and, making its way to the buffalo enclosure, started howling. Terrified, the buffalo broke through their gate and rushed onto the plains.

The notion that some powerful being, back in myth time, was hoarding something that people needed occurs also in stories about natural phenomena. The peoples of the Northwest Coast and the Alaskan Inuit describe how the "keeper of the daylight" kept light in a bag which the Trickster animal, Raven, stole. When Raven pecked the leather bag, daylight streamed forth. The Tlingit and Haida also describe how Raven stole water and sprinkled it over the Earth as he escaped, thus creating the great rivers and lakes of the region.

A widespread myth among the southern farming peoples attributes the origin of corn and beans to a magical woman. The Natchez told how Corn Woman lived with twin girls. Whenever their supplies ran out, Corn Woman went into the corn house and came out with two full baskets. One day, the twins spied on her. Disgusted by the sight of Corn Woman making their food by shaking and rubbing her body, they ran away. Then Corn Woman told them: "From now on you must help yourselves. Kill me and burn my body. When summer comes, plants will come up where you have burned me. These you must cultivate; and when they have grown to maturity, they will be your food."

The emergence myths of the southwestern Pueblo peoples mirror their traditional lives as farmers. Like the first people, corn emerged from a dark underground realm into the light. In this 19th-century Navajo blanket the spirit of corn is flanked by two holy persons.

25

From Darkness to Light

Many of the creation myths that are related by the farming societies of the Southwest tell of the emergence of the first people from a dark subterranean realm out into the sunlight of the Earth's surface. Frequently, this epic upward trail is blazed for human beings by friendly animals and plants. These pioneers are burrowers, climbers and wily strategists such as Coyote and Spider Woman.

"In the Underworld all the people were fools." Thus begins a creation story of the Hopi people from the mesas of the Arizona desert. Like almost all of the Pueblo (village) societies of the Southwest, the Hopi relate origin myths which describe realms, prior to the present world, where people lived before they arrived at their historical homelands. In Hopi myth, as in tales of the neighbouring Zuni, Navajo and Tewa, these earlier realms lay underground: they were places of suffering and darkness in which life became ever more uncomfortable. Most Pueblo creation stories deal with the process of emergence – the long and difficult journey through three or four dark and unsatisfactory underworlds into the sunlight and abundance of the present world's surface.

The earliest Pueblo people were farmers. Before the Spanish arrived in the first half of the sixteenth century, the Zuni and Hopi cultivated beans, corn and squash, in addition to gathering wild plants, and hunting deer and small game. Their necessary preoccupation with the life-giving crops that pushed up through the aridity of the southwestern scrub gave a vivid plausibility to

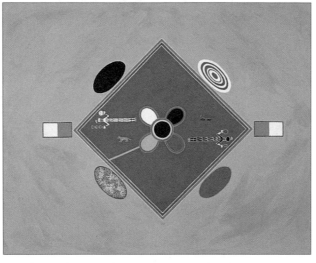

In this sandpainting the Navajo homeland is a square flanked by ovals representing the four sacred mountains. Inside the square are Changing Woman (top), who represents fertility, and White Shell Woman, who represents water. The central circle is the Navajo mythical place of emergence. The line running from the yellow oval represents the reed by which the first people climbed up to the Earth.

mythical images of the first people "coming up" from a deep and dark underworld. So compelling was the symbolism of this magical process that it endured and continued in the belief systems of the Athabascan-speaking Navajo and Apache, who, traditionally, were pastoralists or nomadic hunters and who arrived in the region somewhat later than the crop-raising Pueblo societies.

Like the ceremonies and beliefs of the Pueblo people, these emergence myths are highly complex and detailed. The main participants in the stories are human beings who seek emergence from the underworld, and deities, including the primal creator, the sun god and the twin children of the sun. In addition, two semi-divine beings come to the aid of emerging people: Spider Woman, whose ingenuity, or even her own silk thread, provides a path on the upward journey, and Coyote, a Trickster whose energy and skill help the travellers to overcome obstacles. Animals such as moles, badgers and locusts also play a part in facilitating the epic journey, burrowing through the earth or climbing the plants that rise from the lower to the upper realms.

In the Hopi creation story, "the people were fools" because men and women could not refrain from quarrelling with one another. And when the feuding sexes decided to separate onto opposite banks of a river, their society became sterile. Furthermore, this lower world was unpleasant; it had become contracted; the horizon curved in on it disagreeably; it was dark; and finally it began to flood. Faced with such adversities, the chief of the underworld people did all that he could to find an escape route, a doorway to the sky. He made a prayer stick for Spider Woman, and by this religious act of connection with her, his people earned their ascent to "a good place to go, the good houses".

Spider Woman's role was to facilitate the emergence itself. She did this by breaking down the barrier that existed between the world of darkness and water below and the world of light above. First she planted a spruce tree, but when that failed to penetrate through to the sky, she planted a reed, which finally reached the upper world.

"Alone with the Past", a photograph taken by Roland Reed in the second decade of the 20th century. Two Navajos gaze across the Canyon de Chelly in Arizona at the ruins of an ancient pueblo. Its builders were the Anasazi, prehistoric Pueblo peoples whose surviving dwellings seem to be a part of the landscape.

Various animals then set out on an exploratory ascent. Eventually the locust, carrying his flute, was the first to emerge into the open. There he was immediately attacked by the "Cloud Chiefs" of the four directions. After testing his courage by bombarding him with lightning, the chiefs finally relented, as they had been completely unable to distract him from calmly playing his flute. "You are a good and brave man!" they cried. "Your heart and those of your people must be good. Go tell them to come, and all this land shall be theirs." So the people began their ascent, which took them eight days. When they finally emerged into the upper world, they rejoiced.

The story expresses the Hopi people's religious beliefs: *hopi* itself means "peace" and, in accordance with this, all action within the Hopi world should properly lead to balance, harmony and integration. Their ideal is to live peacefully in a sacramental relationship with all the living things, humans and animals as well as plants, within creation. Thus it is after an act of reverence – the offering of a prayer stick – that the chief and his people come to the upper world.

27

The Search for Home

Emergence myths are common among the Hopi and other Pueblo peoples. However, creation does not end there; no sooner had the first humans emerged than they were faced with another journey. The myths that record their tireless search for a suitable settlement affirm the bond that Pueblo people feel with their ancestral homelands.

The origin myths of the Southwestern Pueblo peoples describe a journey upward through several levels of the underworld to the present sunlit world. Some societies, among them the Hopi, then relate the story of a further migration on earth.

Once the Hopi had emerged from below, supposedly at the confluence of the Colorado and the Little Colorado rivers, Masaw, their guardian spirit, ordered them to travel in the four cardinal directions until they reached the sea, and then to retrace their steps to find their true homeland. Not every clan managed to make its way there, but those who did commemorated their great trek in rock carvings. These rock memorials feature two spiral motifs: square spirals to symbolize the turning back at the seas, and round spirals, to show how the people wandered ever closer to their destination. Over Hopi territory such carved spirals are laid out on the land within an overall shape of a cross, or a swastika with broken arms, which represents the sun's movement. The middle of the cross, *Tuwanasavi,* represents both the centre of the cosmos and the centre of Hopi territory. The Hopi have several ceremonial sites (*kivas*), in the middle of which is an underground circular opening, representing the hole through which the first people emerged into the world.

Between 500 and 1,000 years ago prehistoric North Americans incised the white limestone outcrops of Peterborough County, Ontario, with sacred images. Some North American rock carvings are known to refer to origin beliefs.

Migration stories describing tribal movements since the mythical emergence also abound in the narratives of many other cultures. Sometimes, the main theme of such legends is conflict among tribes, such as that which broke out between the Tewa of northern New Mexico and the Ute of Colorado. Other stories tell how clans of particular tribes, such as the Zuni and Tewa, were guided at several points by helpful spirits. The sacred landmarks where such spirits dwelt are shown on mythical and historical tribal maps.

Why the Snake Clan Lives Apart

Stories such as the migration myth of the Tewa Snake Clan of northern New Mexico explain how groups of people came to revere certain animals – in this case the snake – and to live in particular regions of the country.

Once, a boy of the Tewa lived by a river. Every day he sat by it, saying to himself, "I wonder where this water is running." So one day he cut down a tree to make a box and told his parents that he wanted to go downriver. His uncle made prayer sticks. "If you meet any holy being," said the uncle, "give them prayer sticks." Next morning, the boy sat in the box with his bundle of prayer sticks, and boated down the river.

He travelled until he came to a place with a mountain. As he walked around the mountain a girl came towards him. "I am the one who made you come downriver," she said.

She led him up the mountain, where he found a house with people inside who gave him food. When he finished eating, he glanced round. His hosts looked human, though their skin was yellow and snake-like. But when they went outside, they became snakes. The boy thanked the headman and handed him prayer sticks.

The snake folk showed the boy their dances; they sang their songs and invited him to join them. Soon they asked the boy to marry the girl. Years later, after marrying her and siring several children, the boy was told by his father-in-law: "It is time for you to return to your own people. Your parents miss you. Take your family with you."

When they reached the boy's home they were welcomed. All was well until the snake family's children began to bite the other children in the village. Then, led by the snake woman, the family moved away to the south.

Soon they met other people. "Who are you?" said the snakes. "We are the Sand Clan," said the strangers. "Well, you are my people," said the woman. So they travelled together and met other clans: the Antelope and Tobacco clans, the Lizards, the Bears and the Coyote. That is how the clans of the Tewa met, and some of them joined each other. For example, the Coyote clan and the Antelopes lived together. However, the snakes could not live with other clans, so they settled in the desert.

This buffalo hide painting by a modern Arizona artist depicts the snake clan's mythical migration.

The Great Spirit

A supreme being – variously known as the "Great Spirit", "Father", "Grandfather" or "Old Man" – is for many Native Americans both the creator of the world at the beginning of time and the spirit that presides over and pervades all living things.

The highly complex belief systems of Plains peoples, such as the Pawnee, the Blackfeet and the Sioux, hold all human life to be sacred. For these societies, every human act is imbued with spiritual significance and pays homage to the omnipresent Great Spirit. This transcendent God – Tirawa for the Pawnee, Napi (Old Man) for the Montana Blackfeet, Wakan Tanka (from the word *wakan*, meaning "sacred" or "sacred power") for the Sioux – permeates all people, animals, places and

George Catlin's early 19th-century painting of the *O-kee-pa*, the ceremony by which the Mandans, who lived in riverside earth lodges, connected with the Great Spirit and their mythical past.

phenomena. And while the other spirits who emanate from, or co-exist with, the Great Spirit are also revered, only this supreme deity is regarded as omnipresent and omniscient.

The pantheon of deities revered by the Skidi Pawnee, a Midwestern community of nineteen villages whose beliefs and ceremonies were recorded at the turn of the nineteenth century, is typical of Plains belief systems. These proud people, who were often at war with neighbouring societies and whose men excelled at buffalo and deer hunting, lived in awe of their creator, Tirawa. As the supreme deity, he lived with his spouse, the spirit of the sky-vault, beyond the clouds, and played little or no part in the dynamics of earthly existence. Instead, he ruled through a hierarchy of other spirits. Below Tirawa was the Evening Star, and below him his four assistants, Wind, Cloud, Lightning and Thunder. Morning Star was next in

power, and he was the father of the first human being. Other major forces were the Four Quarters (directions), and the Sun and Moon, the parents of the earth and the providers of such human essentials as hunting equipment. In this cosmos the day-to-day destinies of men and women were determined by animal spirits who came together in sacred lodges to make or mar their fortunes.

The Skidi Pawnee worshipped Tirawa and the lesser spirits in long annual rituals. They acted out the ways of the animals in dance ceremonies as a form of worship and as a means of affirming their power over them in the hunt. Other

The Munificence of the Great Spirit

Although the Native American concept of a benevolent, omniscient and omnipresent god complemented European settlers' idea of one true God, it failed to accord with Wild West propaganda about the savage heathen Indian. Nineteenth- and early twentieth-century European Americans were startled by the tender reverence with which Natives – even the haughtiest and most battle-hardened warriors – regarded the Great Spirit.

The Great Spirit of the Sioux was not summoned at will. Often, his messages were received as powerful visions, or telling dreams, by especially sensitive and responsible individuals.

One such visionary was Brave Buffalo, a Sioux medicine man from North Dakota. His vision of the Great Spirit, which came to him when he was a boy, never left him: "When I was ten years of age I looked at the land and the rivers, the sky above, and the animals around me, and could not fail to realize that they were made by a great power."

Chief Weninock of the Yakimas in eastern Washington State

expressed another dimension of the divine spirit, that of a benevolent provider: "God created Indian country, and it was as if he spread out a great blanket. He put Indians on it.

And all the animals and plants in that country were for the Indian people." In times of upheaval and trauma the Great Spirit offered reassurance and guidance.

This tiny Sioux tipi, made *c.*1830, housed the sacred pipe that was used to make contact with the Great Spirit.

ceremonies, which were always conducted in a great lodge built specially for the purpose, involved the sacred bundle that each village kept as a ritual object. Every village owned a unique bundle given to its ancestors by the Great Spirit. In ceremonies, the bundle was first suspended near the entrance to the lodge and was then taken down for un-wrapping. Village chiefs and holy men supervised the rituals and they, along with the rest of the community, took up positions in the lodge that repro-duced those of the spirits and stars in the firmament.

The Pawnee called their bundles *chuh-rara-peru* (rains-wrapped-up). Their contents varied, but all of them held at least one pipe, and most would contain tobacco, paints, sacred bones and feathers, as well as the maize which Pawnee women cultivated. Laid out in front of the chiefs, the bundles would receive ritual offerings both of smoke from a ceremonial pipe and of buffalo tongues. Until 1818, a human sacrifice in the shape of a girl as a mate for Morning Star was among the offerings. Singing led by holy men and chiefs accompanied these rituals, which were intended to show the community's humility before Tirawa.

Among other Plains Indians, the Great Spirit manifested himself in paradoxical ways. The Old

This late 19th-century Lakota headdress incorporates red trade cloth and glass beads as well as such traditionally prized materials as porcupine quills and eagle feathers.
Such bonnets were the regalia of Plains leaders, whose exploits were numbered in eagle feathers.

Man of the legends of the Blackfeet, for example, is a curious mixture of wis-dom and folly, a Trickster figure who is unpredictably benevo-lent or mean. He also plays pranks and is tricked in turn by puny crea-tures such as squir-rels and mice. In one tale Old Man is playing round a campfire with squirrels; in the course of his game, he gets burned, eats up all the squirrels, fights a lynx and finally inflicts the gashes on the birch tree which it bears to this day. In his more exalted form, Old Man im-parts wisdom to ani-mals and humans.

Like many spirits of Native American wor-ship, the Great Spirit is sometimes represented as a person. But this personification is often vague, and the deity almost always disap-pears from myth after the act of creation. In Hopi myth, the first divinity was Taiowa. At the beginning of time, he created Sotuknang "as a per-son, Taiowa's nephew". It was Sotuknang who would make "life in endless space, and lay out the universes in proper order". Sotuknang proceeded to create nine universal kingdoms, and everything in space and time emerged from his hand. Meanwhile, after the first great act of creation, Taiowa himself retired to one of the worlds made by his nephew and played no further part in mythology. Similar "vanishing creators" feature among the deities of the Navajo, Pima, Apache and other southwestern peoples.

One of the most beautiful accounts of the Great Spirit and of the myths and rituals of the Oglala Sioux comes from the medicine man Black Elk (*c*.1860–1950). Black Elk, who had known such towering figures as Crazy Horse and Sitting Bull, was a veteran of two crucial historical events: the Battle of Little Big Horn in 1876, when General George Armstrong Custer's regiment was wiped out, and the massacre at Wounded Knee in 1890. The nature of the Great Spirit Wakan Tanka is revealed in his story of the visionary experience of two Sioux hunters.

It was dawn as the two men stood on a hill, and towards them came a beautiful young woman dressed in white buffalo robes and with a bundle on her back. When one of the men showed lustful intentions towards the woman, she reduced him to a pile of bones. This *wakan* woman then ordered the other man to return to his village and instruct the chief, Standing Yellow Horn, to build a ceremonial lodge with buffalo skins and twenty-eight poles. After these orders had been carefully carried out, the woman reappeared. Removing the bundle from her back, she said to Standing Yellow Horn, "Behold this bundle and always love it. It is *lela wakan* ('very sacred'), and you must always treat it as such. No impure man should ever be allowed to see it; for within this bundle there is a very holy pipe. With this pipe you will send your voices to Wakan Tanka, your Father and Grandfather, during the years to come. With this sacred pipe you will walk upon the Earth; for the Earth is your grandmother and mother, and she is sacred. Every step that is taken upon her should be as a prayer." The woman then explained that the stone bowl of the pipe, with its carving of a buffalo calf, represented Earth and all the four-footed animals that walked upon it. Its wooden stem stood for all growing things. Twelve Spotted Eagle feathers that hung from the pipe represented all birds. "Whenever you smoke this pipe," the woman said, "all these things join you, everything in the universe: all send their voices to Wakan Tanka, the Great Spirit.

Whenever you pray with this pipe you pray for and with all things."

The ceremonies of the Lakota Sioux enacted the *wakan* woman's injunction to revere the Great Spirit. The pipe ritual was performed in two stages. A dried herb was lit from fire that burned in the centre of the lodge, and the first smoke passed through the pipe-stem and up to heaven. In this way Wakan Tanka was the first to smoke. The pipe was then filled with tobacco and offered in the six sacred directions: west, north, east, south and to heaven and earth. As Black Elk explained: "In this manner, the whole universe is placed in the pipe."

All the components of the pipe ceremonies pointed symbolically to Wakan Tanka as the unifying power of the universe. The ceremonial lodge was constructed to represent that universe. The twenty-eight supporting poles represented the lunar month, and each of the days of this month was sacred: "Two of the days represent the Great Spirit. Two are for Mother Earth; four are for the four winds; one is for the Spotted Eagle; one for the sun; and one for the moon; one is for the Morning Star; and four are for the four ages; seven are for our seven great rites; one is for the buffalo; one is for fire; one for water; one for rock; and, finally, one is for the two-legged people." "The ceremonial lodge," Black Elk explained, "is the centre of the Earth; and this centre, which, in reality, is everywhere, is the dwelling place of Wakan Tanka."

After instructing the Sioux people in their sacred ceremonies, the *wakan* woman walked around the lodge in a clockwise direction. What the lodge-dwellers witnessed as she left confirmed her sanctity: transforming herself into a buffalo, she made a bow in each direction before vanishing from sight.

A 19th-century ceremonial Sioux pipe. The rising smoke from such a pipe was thought of as a path leading to the Great Spirit.

The Origin of the Sun, Moon and Stars

Stories concerning the birth of the sun, moon and stars abound in Native North American mythology. In their cosmologies, different Native peoples emphasized different celestial bodies.

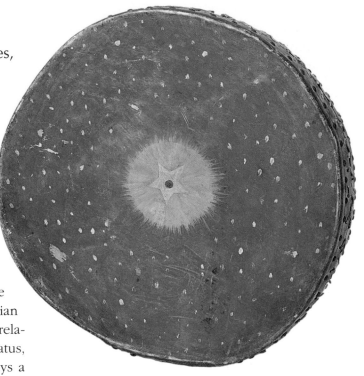

This painted rawhide hand-drum probably belonged to a member of the Ghost Dance religion, which swept through the Plains in the 1890s. It is decorated with stars and dots that symbolize the spirits of the wider cosmos. Through their ceremonies, Ghost Dancers revered the sacred spirits of the sky, whom they saw as allies in the struggle to undo the white men's destruction and restore Native American ways of life.

Among the Blackfeet of northwestern Montana and the Navajo of the southwestern deserts, the sun is seen as much more than just the giver of light: all living and growing things require the energy that is provided by the mighty sun deity. The Cherokee and other Southeastern peoples also worship and propitiate this vital celestial body. By contrast, in the cosmology of the Inuit, as well as among the Tlingit and Tsimshian peoples of the Northwest Coast, the sun is relatively unimportant. As confirmation of this status, the sun is a female in these cultures, and plays a comparatively minor role in myth and belief.

Many of the myths of the Northwest Coast which describe how daylight was created also explain how the stars and moon came into being. These stories usually focus on two main characters, a raven Trickster and a being who hoards the light craved by all living creatures.

A Tlingit myth tells how Raven, part bird, part human, tricked his way into the light-hoarder's house by magically making the man's daughter give birth to himself. And this is how, once he had been born, Raven managed to see the bundles that hung on the walls of his grandfather's house. As the growing raven-baby, he crawled around, weeping and pointing at the bundles. This lasted for some days, until the grandfather cried: "Give my grandchild what he is crying for!" With that the boy was given a bag containing the stars. Rolling it about on the floor, he suddenly released his grip on it and let it float up through the smoke-hole of the house. The stars rose through the sky and scattered, arranging themselves as they have always been since. Raven then repeated his ruse, and the next bag contained the moon.

Daylight, the grandfather's prize possession and the prime object of Raven's desire, was kept in a securely bound box. Knowing by this time that a supernatural force was attacking his household, the grandfather reluctantly ordered the box to be untied. When the raven-baby had the box in his hands and let the daylight out, he uttered his raucous raven cry, "Ga!", and flew up through the chimney. This was how daylight, or sunshine, arrived on the Northwest Coast, together with the moon and the stars.

A Spider's Quest for the Sun

A Cherokee story from the Southeast begins in the shadowy gloom of primordial myth time. In their quest for light, the people are aided by a succession of brave animals.

At first there was no light anywhere, and in the darkness everyone kept bumping into each other. "What we need in the world is light!" they all agreed, and so they convened a meeting. The red-headed woodpecker made a suggestion: "People on the other side of the world have light, so perhaps if we go over there, they will give us some."

After much argument, Possum said: "I'll go and get light. I have a bushy tail and can hide the light inside my fur." So he travelled east, screwing up his eyes against the brightness. When he arrived on the other side of the world, he found the sun, grabbed a piece of it and hid it. But the sun was so hot it burned all the fur from his tail, and when he came home, he had lost the light.

Next, Buzzard went on the quest. On reaching the sun, he dived out of the sky and snatched a piece of it in his claws. Setting it on his head, he started for home, but the sun burned off his head feathers, and Buzzard also lost the light. When Buzzard returned home bald, everyone despaired.

Suddenly they heard a small voice from the grass. "You have done the best a man can do, but perhaps a woman can do better." "Who is that speaking?" the animals shouted. "I am your Grandmother Spider," replied the voice. "Perhaps I was put in the world to bring you light."

Then Spider rolled some clay into a bowl and started towards the sun, leaving a trail of thread behind her. When she was near the sun, she was so little that she wasn't noticed. She reached out gently and took a tiny piece of the sun. Placing it in her bowl, and following the thread she had spun, Spider returned from east to west. And as she travelled, the sun's rays grew and spread before her, across the world.

To this day, spiders' webs are shaped like the sun and its rays. And spiders always spin them in the morning, as if to remind people of their divine ancestor.

Made of buckskin in the shape of a rising sun, this Hopi shield was worn on his back by a priest during a ritual.

The Details of the Universe

While a few stories describe the creation of major celestial bodies, Native American myths more commonly focus on the minutiae of the universe. Thus, one Lillooet story explains the moon's irregular surface in terms of the presence of three squatting frog sisters. Similarly, the star cluster known as the Pleiades is seen in an Iroquois myth as a band of children dancing at night.

"In the beginning the Great Medicine created the Earth, and the waters upon the Earth, and the sun, moon and stars." The creation story of the Cheyenne from the Plains, which opens with these words, proceeds to human beginnings without further mention of the origin of the cosmos. In some Indian cultures, this treatment of the celestial lights is preceded by a quiet, poetic vision of how things were at the beginning of time. Once the origins of sun and moon have been mentioned, the narrative often hurries on to a description of life on Earth and legends of the first people. The Lenape of Delaware have one such story: a deity known as Kishelamakank, at the very beginning of time, existed alone in space and silence. Suddenly he had a vision: he saw space filled with stars, sun, moon and Earth. Then, in keeping with his vision, the Earth sprang to life, followed by human existence in all its variety. But one god's thought was not enough to create the universe. The lonely creator therefore summoned help for his great task. He brought into being four Keepers of Creation and with these four spirits he conspired to produce the stars, sun, moon and Earth. Gathering strength, as if by chain reaction, the sun with its heat and the moon with her powers of fertility then brought life to the world. Once this had been accomplished, the Lenape creation story moves on to a description of "things as they are and have always been". The world of people and nature takes over.

If large cosmological events are sometimes passed over, what may seem minor aspects of creation are often explained in rather elaborate detail. Thus, a myth of the Lillooet of the Northwest Coast describes how three Frog Sisters refused the advances of the Beaver and Snake who came to court them. Beaver's disappointed weeping brought on rain. Threatened with a flood, the sisters escaped to the house of the moon. When the moon invited them to warm themselves by the fire, they insisted on sitting on his head. Jumping onto the moon's face, they spoiled his then unblemished beauty, and are still there to this day.

Similarly, the precise position of the sun is the subject of a Navajo creation myth. When "the first people" have arrived at their final home, the Sun Man and Moon Man who have accompanied them on their ascent to the "fifth world" are hurled by the first people into the sky. The sun, which at first burns too hot, gradually withdraws as the people

Morning Star, a deity who was associated with the well-being of humanity, decorates the headrest of this 19th-century cradleboard from the Plains. The board would have served as the frame for a buckskin baby carrier.

The board around the "face" of this 19th-century Inuit dance
mask represents the air; the hoops are the different levels, or
layers, of the cosmos; and the feathers are the stars.

make sacrifices to the power of heat and light. Thereafter, the sun moves in an orderly way from east to west every day, and the moon reigns over the night sky.

Perhaps because stars appear to be arranged in orderly groups, Native American myths sometimes describe particular groups of them as families or little societies. The seven stars that make up the Pleiades have inspired many origin myths. One story, told by the Onondaga, an Iroquoian society of New York State, relates how a group of people settled in a favourite hunting area. The place was particularly pleasant, game was plentiful, and while the adults constructed their lodges, the children organized some dances of their own.

Time passed and the children continued to dance every day. One day, however, a strange old man appeared and ordered them to stop. But they did not obey his instruction and kept on dancing. Then a small boy suggested that, next time they met, they should bring food from their parents' lodges and enjoy a feast together. But their parents refused their request. Undaunted, the children continued their merry-making, still happy though hungry. Then one day as they danced, light-headed with hunger, they found themselves rising up into the sky. "Don't look back," their leader warned them. As they floated up, their parents ran out of their lodges laden with food to tempt the children back to earth. But it was too late. One child who glanced down became a shooting star. The others, when they had ascended to the heavens, became the Pleiades star cluster: a band of happy children dancing through the night.

37

The Peopling of the Earth

Often, the first people are essentially no different from animals. Both share the same food and land and speak the same language. Some myths tell of this early time as an age without sickness and death when life is perfect, until a Trickster like Raven or Coyote changes things, and makes life as later humans have always known it.

An Alaskan Inuit story begins: "Raven man harpooned the land. It came up from the water. And there was a small dwelling there with a man and woman in it." People, the story suggests, were simply there all the time, from the beginning of creation. A similar view is expressed in stories of the northeastern Winnebago Indians. In many such origin tales, people, animals and a semi-divine Trickster all live together at the beginning of time. And while people and animals may take on different roles in particular stories, human and animal natures are not essentially different from each other. At the dawn of time the beings who existed combined human nature with that of the creatures whom later Native Americans knew and often hunted. This vision of the first people is sometimes set in a blank and featureless landscape, such as the one which the Alaskan Raven created, and sometimes in a primeval world presided over by a god-like creator. In this world, often half water and half land, the creator thinks, dreams or sings the people into existence.

Many Native American cultures portray a world in which people are made before anything else comes into being; in others, human beings are made at the end of a long process involving the creation of plants, animals and natural features. The early people described by the Cheyenne of the Plains are placed by their creator, Great Medicine, in a "beautiful country" where people, animals and birds "who were all friends and had a common language" came into being at more or less the same time. The people went naked and were never hungry until the Earth was struck by floods and earthquakes. The ancestors were then forced to dress in skins and hunt for their food. Great Medicine eventually took pity and brought them corn to plant and buffalo to hunt. This paradisal Cheyenne dream time is, however, a type rare in Native American myth, and may have been influenced by Christian ideas.

Many origin stories describe the first people as helpless beings, physically deficient or technologically naïve. In some myths an all-powerful creator brings people to perfection; in others, the people have to sort themselves out, or their survival depends on the outcome of a struggle between rival spirits.

The origin myths of the Blackfeet of the Plains describe how people were made by Old Man, the master spirit who "travelled around making things as he went". The first people he created were a woman and child, whom he fashioned from clay. They were poor and naked. Old Man had to teach them how to gather food and hunt. However, the people had no arms and the buffalo would chase them. Scornful of the people's timidity, Old Man gave them arms and taught them to make weapons. From this time on, they were able to hunt the buffalo for food and leather.

The shape of early people was not finally determined. A story from the

This ancient Inuit comb (c.500BC) is incised with an image of an archer standing over a prostrate man and a variety of animals. The archer may represent a mythical creator god.

38

The Giver and the Watcher

According to this Tututni myth from southwest Oregon, two creative beings, the Giver and the Watcher, emerged from the purifying steam of their sweat lodge to collaborate in the making of humanity.

In the beginning there was no land. The Giver and the Watcher sat outside their sweat lodge. One day the Watcher saw land beginning to emerge from the waters which surrounded them. The Giver took some tobacco. He smoked and the land became solid. Five times the Giver smoked and discussed how the world and people might be made. He worked for days. Then day and night came, trees and grass appeared and the ocean withdrew.

Now it was time to make the first people. The Giver took some grass, mixed it with mud and rubbed it in his hands and made two figures. After four days two dogs, one male and one female, appeared, and the dogs bore a litter. Then the Giver went to work again. He fashioned two figures out of sand. This time the Giver had made snakes.

Soon the Giver thought, "How can I make people? I've failed twice!" The Watcher spoke, "Let me smoke tonight, and see if people emerge from smoke." For three days he smoked, and from the smoke a house appeared with smoke coming from it. After a while, a beautiful woman emerged. The Giver was glad, and said: "Now we'll have no trouble making people." The

woman could not see the Giver and Watcher. But after nine days she grew sad and wondered who her kinsfolk were.

One day the Giver said to his companion: "Stay here and take this woman to wife. You shall have children and be father of all people. I'm leaving this world. Everything on it shall belong to you." The woman became pregnant. Even then she still couldn't see her husband, and when her son was born, she still did not know his father. So she wrapped up her child and went on a journey.

The woman and her son travelled for ten years. At last the boy asked, "Mother, where is your husband?" She replied: "I've dreamed of my husband." Then the Giver said to his companion: "The woman is home now."

At dusk the next day the Watcher, now a man, came in and the boy exclaimed: "My father has come!" The Watcher duly told them all that had happened. Meanwhile, the Giver brought order to the world and made the animals. He told the couple to have many children: "You, your wife and children shall speak many tongues. You'll be the parents of all the tribes."

In the 1820s the artist George Catlin recorded buffalo hunting,
a way of life that was all but extinct within another 50 years.

Yana of northern California says that the gender of the first people was changeable. There were just thirty women and thirty men. The men went out deer hunting while the women pounded acorns for bread. The men returned home from hunting with nothing. "What shall we do?" the women said. "There is no meat. Let us make women from men, and men from women." So it happened. The new men went out hunting and killed many deer, while the new women stayed at home and pounded acorns. In that way they prospered. Their numbers grew. But Coyote, the Trickster, did not like it. "There are too many women and too many men!"

Opposed to Coyote were Cottontail Rabbit, Grey Squirrel and Lizard. They knew about death but did not want it to be final, and they argued (see page 43) with Coyote about whether it should be allowed to claim people. The animals then had another disagreement with Coyote about hands. In those days people's hands were round and fingerless, like Coyote's. "Let us cut through their hands," said Lizard. "They need fingers to shoot arrows and to pound sunflower seeds and acorns." "They can use their elbows," said Coyote. "Why do you talk about changing things?"

"We don't like them as they are," said Lizard and Rabbit. Then Lizard went off and sat in the sun. He leaned against a rock and, picking up a flint, he cut through his hands, making fingers. "Well, well!" whispered everyone when Lizard showed them his hands. Then he fixed their hands too. Now they could hunt deer with arrows of flint; they could fish for salmon and pound acorns. "When women have children," Lizard said, "they'll all have fingers." Only Coyote had no fingers. He sat by the sweat lodge hanging his head.

The First People of Northern California

The Californian Kato people believed that the creator named Nagaitcho did not rest from his labours until he was sure that the Earth had resources enough to sustain the first people.

Two creative spirits, Nagaitcho and Thunder, presided over an ageing cosmos that was devoid both of people and of all the living and growing things on which they depend. Even the sandstone rock which formed the sky was old. Thunder raged in the four directions. "The rock is old," Nagaitcho said to him, "we will fix it."

They stretched out the sky and walked on it. Then gates and trails were put in place. They made a hole in the sky to let the clouds and fog through. They made the clouds so that the heads of the people to come wouldn't ache from bright sun.

Nagaitcho made a man out of earth. He made a left leg and a right leg, and then a left arm and a right arm. Then he pulled up some grass and, forming it into a wad, he made the belly. Then he slapped some grass together and made the heart. He moulded a round piece of clay into a liver. With more clay he made lungs and kidneys. He pushed in a reed for the trachea. "What will the blood be?" he then asked himself. He pounded some ochre and mixed it with water. Next he made the mouth, nose and eyes. "Now the genitals," he

said. And having made the male genitals, he took one of the legs, split it and made a woman from it.

The story continues with a detailed description of the creation of the things that the new people needed for existence in their country. Edible seaweeds and mussels came from the sea. "What will be salt?" Nagaitcho wondered. The ocean foam was turned into salt. The Indians tried it and decided to use it on their food in future.

Next, Nagaitcho began a tour of the land with his dog. They surveyed the beautiful landscape of redwood, oak and chestnut trees, springs, creeks, hills and valleys. Animals, large and small, quenched their thirst in the waters that they shared with people. "I have made a good earth, my dog," said the creator. The nuts and berries and grasses were ripe. Fish for people swam in the streams. All kinds of edible things had grown in abundance. Nagaitcho's first people had found their home and lived there in harmony.

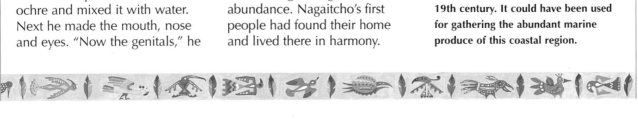

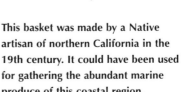

This basket was made by a Native artisan of northern California in the 19th century. It could have been used for gathering the abundant marine produce of this coastal region.

How Old Age and Death Began

While many Native American creation stories take the cycle of life, from birth to death, as a given fact, not all of them accept that, from the beginning, mortality was inevitable. A story told by the Modoc people of northern California describes how five brothers who went on a killing spree were responsible for bringing old age to the world.

Rampaging across the land, five brothers murdered everyone they met. Eventually their reputation spread so far that people fled to the wilderness at the news of their approach. The brothers therefore found no one in the north, the south and west: but when they arrived in the eastern quarter, they came upon an old man and an old woman. "We have come to fight you," the brothers said. "But we don't want to fight," said the old people. "Go away and leave us alone."

The brothers refused to listen and started to attack. They shot the old man with arrows and beat him with clubs. They built a fire and tried to burn him. But when they found that they could not kill him, the brothers grew frightened and ran off, with the two old people in pursuit. "Stop!" shouted the old man. The brothers did not heed his warning, so the old man and woman ran faster and caught up with them.

Straight away, the oldest brother grew old and weak. He stumbled on a little way further and then fell dead. This happened to each of the five brothers in turn. "And that", according to this Modoc story, "is how old age came into our world. If those brothers had left the old people alone, there would be no such thing as old age."

In other Native American stories, death comes not at the very beginning of creation, but a little later – though still in mythical time. At the outset, all of the people and all of the animals are immortal. But then some accident happens: someone does something wrong without knowing it, and then death arrives. One tale from the Tahltan people of the Northwest Coast describes a Tree Woman and a Rock Woman, both of whom are pregnant. Rock Woman does not follow the correct child-bearing procedure, and her baby, half-born, turns completely to rock and then dies. Afterwards, although Tree Woman successfully gives birth to her child, the mortality of people is a fact of life: "People are like trees. Some will live long and some will die young. Thus death comes to people of all ages, just as among trees, and none can live very long."

Roland Reed's 1912 photograph of a Blackfoot burial platform. The body is raised up to protect it from scavengers and to bring it near the spirits of the sky.

Coyote and the Origin of Death

According to this tale, which is told by the Caddo people of Arkansas, death would have been only a temporary interlude if the Trickster, Coyote, had not decided that it should be final. He came to this decision in order to protect those living from scarcity.

In the beginning there was no death. Everyone lived until there were so many people that there was no more room on earth. So the chiefs held a council, and one man said that people should die, but just for a while, and then they should come back again. Then Coyote jumped up, declaring that people should die for ever. The world was not big enough to hold all those people and if they came back to life, there would not be sufficient food to sustain everyone.

It was decided that the village medicine men should build a grass house facing east and place a black and white eagle feather on top of it. When anyone died, the feather would become bloody and fall over. Then the medicine men would sit in the house and sing: this would call the spirit of the dead person, so that he or she would live again.

After a time, the first feather grew bloody and fell over. The medicine men gathered, and after some days a whirlwind blew in from the west, circled the house and entered it from the east. Once the wind was in the house a fine young man who had recently been killed emerged. Everyone was happy, except Coyote. So next time the feather grew bloody and fell from the roof, and the whirlwind circled the house of grass, Coyote closed the door. The spirit in the whirlwind, finding the door closed, swept on by. From that moment on, death became final.

When Coyote saw what he had done, he was afraid. Since then he has run from place to place, for ever glancing behind him to see if he is being chased. And when anyone hears the wind whistle, they say: "There's someone, a spirit, wandering about!" Now, the spirits of the dead must wander the earth before they find the spirit land.

MYTH AND ART

The rich art of Native North American cultures expresses their connection with the spiritual world, particularly with the animals they regarded as their ancestors and kin. Supernatural spirits, symbols and patterns were carved, painted, woven or sewn onto everyday utensils, garments, house fronts and boats, as well as in sacred and ceremonial objects such as masks, totem poles and pipes. Myth was inseparable from daily routine, and decorations represented, among other themes, thanks to the spirits, protection in warfare, or accompaniment on a spiritual journey.

Above: Elaborately carved and painted masks of the Northwest Coast – such as this bold-eyed Kwakiutl head – commemorated the ancestors of clans and families. Masked dancers also celebrated victories over a human, animal or supernatural adversary.

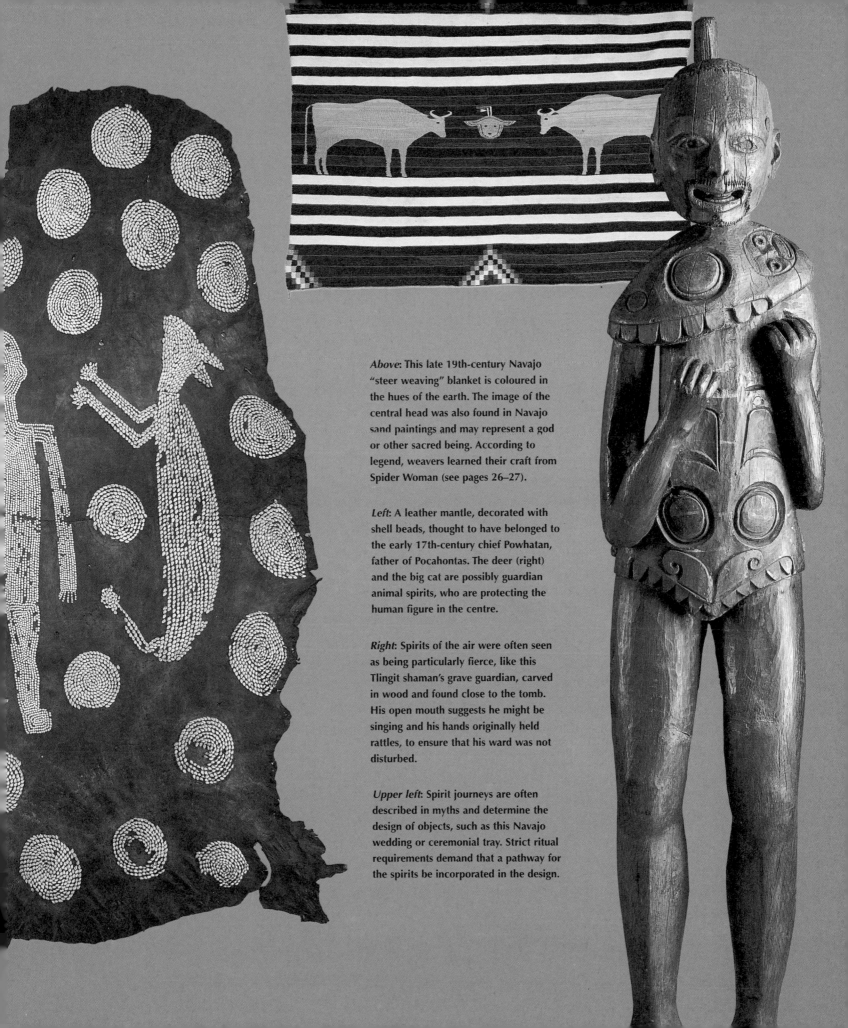

Above: This late 19th-century Navajo "steer weaving" blanket is coloured in the hues of the earth. The image of the central head was also found in Navajo sand paintings and may represent a god or other sacred being. According to legend, weavers learned their craft from Spider Woman (see pages 26–27).

Left: A leather mantle, decorated with shell beads, thought to have belonged to the early 17th-century chief Powhatan, father of Pocahontas. The deer (right) and the big cat are possibly guardian animal spirits, who are protecting the human figure in the centre.

Right: Spirits of the air were often seen as being particularly fierce, like this Tlingit shaman's grave guardian, carved in wood and found close to the tomb. His open mouth suggests he might be singing and his hands originally held rattles, to ensure that his ward was not disturbed.

Upper left: Spirit journeys are often described in myths and determine the design of objects, such as this Navajo wedding or ceremonial tray. Strict ritual requirements demand that a pathway for the spirits be incorporated in the design.

THE SPIRITUAL COSMOS

"The Great Spirit is our Father, but the Earth is our Mother. She nourishes us; that which we put into the ground she returns to us ..." (Big Thunder, Wabanakis nation, Maine). "The country knows. If you do wrong things to it, the whole country knows. It feels what's happening to it. I guess everything is connected together somehow ..." (Koyukon Indian, central Alaska). "What is life? It is the flash of a firefly in the night. It is the breath of a buffalo in the winter time. It is the little shadow which runs across the grass and loses itself in the sunset." (1890, the last words of Crowfoot, Blackfoot warrior.)

These words were spoken by men from three very different Indian societies, but they bear eloquent testimony to an awareness of the cosmos that is shared by all Native American cultures. This cosmos recognizes no separation between the spiritual and the material, between the real and the supernatural, or between the animate and the inanimate, because everything and everyone is endowed with spirit power, or "medicine". When Big Thunder referred to the Great Spirit as a father and the Earth as a mother, he was describing a spiritual kinship, a relationship between humanity and the universe that is not negotiable. The notion of owning anything that comes from the land is as absurd as it is presumptuous. To live on the Earth, to breathe and drink and feed from its resources, and to be among the plants and animals, is to be part of a sacred cosmic unity.

The Earth itself is holy, with a sacred history that explains how the first people came into being, and how each tribe came to occupy its particular place on the land. The animals on which humans depend for food and warmth have the same spiritual value as their hunters. They are companion species and their spirits must be acknowledged and respected, even when they are dead. The sky is a part of the cosmos, and as such it is crowded with spirits, the spirits of the sun and the moon and the stars, the spirits of the wind and the sea. Every natural phenomenon – forests, mountains, rocks, rivers, lakes, plants – has its spirit. Myths tell of the diverse origins of different spirit "personalities" – the behaviour of the sun, the rhythms of the seasons, the movements of animals – but cosmic harmony depends on a balance being struck between these. Through stories, rituals and ceremonies, Native Americans reveal and affirm their kinship with the sacred totality.

Above: **For the Kiowa of Wyoming the shaft of rock known as the Devil's Tower is linked by myth with the power of the Great Spirit.**

Left: **The Grand Canyon, Arizona, a natural marvel with sacred meaning in the mythologies of the Pueblo peoples.**

"The Earth is my Mother"

Native American stories about the origins of the Earth are as various as the peoples, but from the east to the west coast, and from north to south, there is unanimous agreement on the sanctity of the Earth. Within the extended family of kindred spirits that constitutes the Native American cosmos, the bountiful Earth is often likened to a mother. The numerous myths and rituals that surround this figure bear witness to an ancient and indissoluble sense of kinship.

Every phenomenon and every aspect of creation within the Native American cosmos has a spiritual dimension, but the Earth, which is home to all living and growing things, is regarded as having special sanctity.

Stories show this mythical Earth Mother as having many faces, as numerous as her diverse landscapes, and all of her children affirm their kinship with her. Early in the nineteenth century, the visionary Shawnee chief Tecumseh tried to rally a number of tribes against the white men's incursions. In 1811, he declared: "The sun is my father, and the Earth is my mother; on her bosom I will

The Great Serpent Mound, a huge coiling earthwork, was built over 2000 years ago by an Ohio valley culture. It has been seen as affirming the Native tradition of reverence for the Earth.

rest." Tecumseh saw himself as an Indian first, and a Shawnee second, and when he spoke of the Earth as his kin, he was speaking on behalf of every Native American.

Many stories about the Earth's creation explain how this came to be so. In Algonquian tradition, the Earth was created by Gluskap, a mythic hero who made the whole known world from the body of his own mother. Similarly, the Oglala

Sioux, who often speak of the Great Spirit, Wakan Tanka, as the grandfather of all things, also speak of the Earth as the grandmother of all things. Some mythologies provide this female Earth with a mate. For the Yuma people of the southern California desert the Earth's husband is the sky. After a primal embrace between the earth woman and the sky man, the Earth conceived and gave birth to twin sons. As their first task, the twins rose up from their mother's body to lift up the sky.

Away from the desert, the divine geometry of the world is less readily imagined as a division between Earth and sky. In the myths of the Algonquian peoples of the northeastern woodlands, the cosmos is pictured as a sequence of realms. Flat Earth is surmounted by a world of winds and clouds. Above it is the circle of the upper sky, where the Great Spirit dwells. But the sky is only the floor of the topmost heavenly world, which contains representations of all the things that exist beneath it. And the Earth below is the roof of an underworld, from which emerge the waters and plants that sustain life.

As they saw the immigrants' frontier creep ever further west, Native Americans defended the integrity of their sacred Earth against alien ways. In the 1850s, Smohalla, the Wanapum holy man whose prophecies anticipated the Ghost Dance movement of the Plains (see page 130), reminded his people of their sacred pact with the Earth. To save themselves from ruin, Smohalla's followers had to refuse the white men's ways. When the

The Sacred Home of the Choctaw

This story from the Lower Mississippi tells how the Choctaw people, when they had to move their village, not only established a new connection with the Earth, but were guided in their search by the Earth itself.

The Choctaw elders gathered and at length they chose two men, twins, who would lead them forward into new territory. But first a shaman told these men to cut a young, slender tree, and to strip it down until it was a pole. Then the shaman painted it and set it in the earth. "Whichever direction the stick points in the morning," said the holy man, "there you must travel." The following day, the stick was leaning towards the southeast and so the people began their journey in that direction, taking the pole with them. For years they travelled. Children were born and people died. And the remains of those who died on the way were carried in pots to their future settlement. Every night the people set up the pole, and every morning they consulted it. One morning, the pole stood upright, so then the people knew they had reached the land where they should settle.

A painting by Paul Kane (1810–71) of an Indian village. Spiritual concerns influenced the choice of a camp site.

"And where," they wondered, "shall we leave the remains of our loved ones?" "Let us place them in this sacred mound of earth," the twins said. "The place of the Fruitful Mound is our home for ever."

That was how the Choctaws' sacred place came to be at Nanih Waya – at least until the whites took their land by the River Beyond Age, the Mississippi.

49

white men ploughed and mined and fenced the land, they were not simply destroying Native American habitats, they were murdering a cherished body. "You ask me to plough the ground! Shall I take a knife and tear my mother's bosom? You ask me to dig for stone! Shall I dig under her skin for bones? You ask me to cut grass and make hay and sell and be rich like the white men! But how dare I cut off my mother's hair?"

A similar anguish caused the leader of another people, Young Chief of the Cayuses in Washington Territory, to ask: "I wonder if the ground has anything to say? I hear what the ground says. The ground says, 'It is the Great Spirit that placed me here. The Great Spirit tells me to take care of the Indians, to feed them properly.' The water says the same thing. The grass says the same thing. 'Feed the Indians well,' the ground says, 'the Great Spirit has placed me here to

produce all that grows on me, trees and fruit.' In the same way the ground says, 'It was from me man was made. The Great Spirit in placing men on earth, desired them to take good care of the ground and to do each other no harm …'".

Again and again, the Native American belief in the indivisibility of land and human existence is proclaimed. In 1900, nearly a century after Tecumseh's testimony, Big Thunder of the northeastern Wabanakis nation declared: "The Great Spirit is our Father, but the earth is our Mother. She nourishes us; that which we put into the ground, she returns to us, and healing plants she gives us likewise. If we are wounded we go to our mother to lay the wounded part against her to be healed." History rode roughshod over the landscape of Native America, but in the myths and ritual that continue to tell of its sacred past, the Earth lives on as the ultimate cosmic gift.

Sunset glows over the marshland of Bosque del Apache National Wildlife Park in New Mexico. The Native American attitude to the natural world is highly complex. Landscapes and skyscapes are not merely suffused with beauty; they also form part of the spiritual cosmos.

Old Man Arranges the World

Some myths describe how the Earth's sacred identity derives from the fact that the creator was once physically present. The mountainous western landscape of the Blackfeet bears the imprint of Napi, "Old Man", the mythical creator of the Earth.

The Blackfoot origin story tells of Old Man moving through primal territory, creating the features and inhabitants of the rugged mountainous land that was to become the cherished homeland of the Blackfoot nation.

All animals of the Plains at one time knew Old Man. He came from the south. He made the mountains, prairies, timber and brush. So he travelled, arranging the world as we see it today. Everywhere that Old Man went, he made new things. And all these things were connected to each other and were mutually useful. Old Man covered the Plains with grass for the animals. And when things were not quite right, he was prepared to adjust them. The prairies, for example, didn't suit the ways of the bighorn. So Old Man took those animals by the horns and led them to the mountains. "This is the place that suits you," he said. He did the same when he made the antelope, leading them down from their first home in the mountains to the prairie. In this way, particular terrains and the creatures living upon them became suited to one another.

As he went about his primal, earth-moving and animal-arranging labours, the Old Man of the Blackfeet was often challenged by other great spirits, such as those of the sun and thunder, but his engaging and agreeable personality won through. He liked to rest from his labours every now and then, and had a keen sense of humour. A lighthearted episode in the Blackfoot origin story describes how the creator sat on a steep hill top and surveyed with some satisfaction the country he had made. "Well, this is a fine place for sliding," he mused, "I'll have some fun." He promptly began to slide down the hill; the marks he made while doing so can still be seen today at Old Man's Sliding Ground in Montana.

The Circle of Heaven

The celestial world of Native belief systems is alive with spirits, which manifest themselves as night and day or as changes in the weather and the seasons. Many myths reveal the origins of these sky spirits, their place in creation and the parts they play in life on Earth.

The mythical firmament of Native North America has a variety of "geographies". For Californian peoples, the sky is like a roof, supported by pillars of rock which sometimes collapse with age and wreak havoc on earth, whereas, for the Ojibway and the Pueblo peoples, the upper world is a sequence of layers, one above the other.

The Pawnee people of the Plains have a highly detailed conception of the firmament. The sky world that is described in their myths consists of three layers, or circles. At the level of the clouds is the "circle of visions". Above that is the "circle of the sun"; and, highest of all, is the circle of Tirawa, or "Father Heaven". Tirawa, the Great Spirit who created and informs every other spirit, is the husband of the female spirit who presides over the vault of the sky.

Before he made people, Tirawa specified the place and purpose of each heavenly body. The sun and the "Great Star" of morning (Venus) were placed in the east; the moon and the "Bright Star" of evening (again, Venus) were located in the west. The pole star, in the north, was ordained by Tirawa as the "Star-chief of the Skies", while the

This Tsimshian mask has a moon face. The moon is important in all Native American mythologies, but in those of the Tsimshian and other peoples of the Northwest Coast it is understood to be the major source of light.

"Spirit-star" (Sirius), which was designed to be occasionally visible, was placed in the south. The four stars of the quartered regions – northeast, northwest, southeast and southwest – were positioned so as to hold up the heavens. Tirawa's stars were also required to manage other phenomena – the spirits of clouds, winds, lightning and thunder. Having given these forces their roles, Tirawa dropped a pebble into their midst. It rolled about in the clouds and then the waters of the lower world appeared. It was from these waters that the Earth itself emerged.

The Pawnee conception of a balanced hierarchy of celestial spirits contrasts with the dense sky world of the Cherokee. Cherokee myths tell of a sky made of rock, above which live the spirits of thunder .

The sun, as in Pawnee myth, lives in the east, the moon in the west. Above the sky vault dwells the Great Thunderer and his two Thunder Boys, beautifully garbed in lightning and the rainbow. Other thunder spirits inhabit the mountains and cliffs of the sky; they travel on invisible bridges from mountain to mountain where they have their houses. Some of these auxiliary thunder

The War with the Sky Folk

According to this story, which was told by the Kathlamet people of the Northwest Coast, the unruly spirits who lived in the primal sky plagued the first inhabitants of the Earth with destructive storms. Eventually, their victims decided to retaliate.

Below on Earth, in the early time when people and animals were one and spoke the same language, tempests were perpetually wrecking houses and canoes, and making everyone miserable. So Blue Jay said: "We will sing the sky down." He sang for five years, but nothing happened. "Call all the people!" Blue Jay ordered. They all sang incessantly, but the sky did not move. At last Snow Bird began singing. The sky began to tilt. It tilted till it touched the earth. They fastened it to Earth and all the people climbed up into the sky.

Once in the sky, the animals began to wage war against the sky folk. By cutting the bow-strings of their enemy, they routed the sky warriors. Then, headed by Eagle, the birds of prey attacked the southwest winds. The four elder winds were killed by the birds, but the youngest, the wind of the southwest, escaped – the only survivor. Their mission accomplished, most of the invaders returned home and the sky sprang back into place. But some of those who had ascended remained in the sky: Woodpecker, Skate, Elk and Deer stayed there and became stars.

This richly carved and painted pole, the work of a Northwest Coast Haida sculptor, depicts Thunderbird. A sky-dweller imbued with great power, Thunderbird was widely believed to have been instrumental in creation.

spirits are benign, responsive to prayers and appeals from people, but other weather spirits are less sympathetic. According to some Cherokee storytellers, the moon is a ball that was thrown into the sky in a mythical game. Long ago two villages were playing against one another when the leader of one team broke the rules that forbade contact between hand and ball, and picked it up. Trying to throw it into goal, he tossed it so high that it hit the solid sky and stuck there as a reminder not to cheat.

For the Cherokee, the sky-vault was not only solid, but came down to the ground at "the sunrise place" where it could be touched. Once, a party of young men decided to visit this place and gain access to the sky. They travelled east for a long time and eventually reached the spot where the sky meets the ground. There they found that the sky was a dome of solid rock that was suspended above the Earth and swung up and down. Each time it swung up, an opening appeared, which promptly closed as the dome swung down again. At sunrise, the sun appeared through this gap and proceeded to rise up the inside of the dome. The young men had waited for this moment to climb up on to the outside of the dome. But the first to attempt the feat was crushed by a falling rock. The others gave up and began their long trek home.

Watery Realms

In the mythologies of Native America any great body of water – be it the sea, a lake, or a river – is likely to be imbued with spiritual power. This power may belong to the water itself, or to the life-giving fish or sea mammals it contains.

According to a number of stories about the creation of the world, *terra firma* arose from primal waters (see page 21). Other myths describe later floods, like the flood that faced Noah in Judaeo-Christian tradition, which are visited upon the earth by vengeful deities or spirits. The Caddo people of the southeastern Plains speak of a mythical time when the waters of the Earth dried up. On seeing this, the people said: "The river animals and fish have made this drought happen." Crazed by thirst, they picked dead fish and turtles from the river beds, cut them into pieces and threw them around. This foolish behaviour incurred the wrath of a sky spirit, who came down to Earth and punished them by causing a flood. Then the spirit led a small group of people up to the summit of a high mountain, and these survivors were joined, when the waters receded, by other people whom the great flood had transformed into alligators.

The Salmon People

The waters of the Northwest Coast teem with an abundance of fish and sea mammals, and the traditions of the coastal peoples acknowledge a host of marine spirits. The Haida's mythical account of their own origins begins on the sea shore. One day, when the trickster deity, Raven, was scavenging on the shore, he saw a human face peeking out of a partly opened clamshell. Curious, and eager for company, he pecked it open and the first Haida clambered on to dry land.

No marine creature was more important than the salmon, which, during the summer months, makes spawning runs up every inlet of the Northwest Coast. The five types of salmon – chinook, sockeye, humpback, coho and dog salmon – were perceived as five distinct clans of salmon "people". For most of the year these salmon folk looked human and they lived in underwater communities beyond the horizon. Each spring, the salmon clans left their underwater lodges and sailed up inlets and rivers to their summer spawning grounds, where they allowed themselves to be caught as fish. Although all of the salmon clans set out together, the troublesome dog salmon were inclined to capsize the canoes of the coho; this myth explains why this particular species of salmon arrives later than the others. The generosity of the salmon people, in allowing their bodies to be caught and eaten by humans, was appreciated in the harvest rituals of the peoples of the

The spirit of the octopus is invoked in this spectacular Tlingit mask. It was found in the grave of an Alaskan shaman.

Northwest Coast. If the spirits of the salmon people were suitably honoured, they would be willing to be born again as fish. The Tsimshian performed salmon-welcoming ceremonies and the Nootka reverently returned the bones of the first salmon catch to the water.

Besides containing life-sustaining creatures such as salmon, seals and whales, the waters of the Northwest Coast were believed to harbour monstrous mythical beings who were responsible for storms and tides. One such beast is Sisiutl, the giant two-headed serpent of Kwakiutl lore. Sisiutl guards the underwater villages of other marine spirits, and devours any human who dares to venture close to them. He is equally at home on land and in water, and may sometimes take the form of a canoe that can propel itself along and devour seals. In many stories Sisiutl engages in battle with the Thunderbird (see pages 64–65)

In seeking to manage the unpredictable power of the sea, Inuit shamans relied on the friendly spirits of familiar animals. This carved walrus may have served as an amulet or charm for the protection of seafarers.

The Power of the Sea

Among the sea myths of Native America, those of the Canadian Inuit are unique in that they describe an all-powerful deity. Like the sea itself, this deity, personified as the goddess Nuliayuk, is both kind and forbidding, generous and destructive. Nuliayuk's story begins as a tragedy. As a marriageable young woman, she refused to take a husband and was banished by her father to an island. Her father eventually relented and went to bring her home. As they returned, however, a storm blew up. Her father blamed this misfortune on Nuliayuk and threw his daughter overboard. As she clung to the boat's gunwale, he severed her fingers, which were transformed into the great sea mammals. Nuliayuk descended to the sea bed where for ever more she exercised control over the sea creatures. Thereafter, the welfare of all coastal Inuit depended on Nuliayuk's goodwill. When she was pleased with the way people were living, she provided ample game from the sea, but when people offended her by breaking taboos, she withheld the animals and shamans had to travel to the sea bed to bargain for the release of game. Other versions of this myth refer to the sea goddess as Sedna or Takanakapsaluk (see page 117).

There were, of course, many Native American societies that had no experience of the sea. Migration stories told by the desert peoples of the Southwest sometimes speak of the ocean as "the water with one shore". This awareness of the sea was either transmitted by hearsay, or came from distant generations that had migrated inland long before. Papago men of south-central Arizona used to make an annual pilgrimage to the Gulf of California to gather salt. Before they could return home with the salt deposits that they gathered on the beaches, the men had to enter the sea and offer prayer sticks and handfuls of corn to this alien power. To enter the sea at all was regarded by these non-swimmers as an act of heroism, and anything they gathered as they stood in the water, such as seaweed or driftwood, became an amulet of special power. Those who returned from the ordeal enjoyed enhanced status and frequently became shamans. Special songs and orations were composed to commemorate their experience: "I sprinkled corn meal as I ran into the wide-spreading water," runs one song. "Though it crashed dangerously toward me, I did not heed it. But I walked near and cast the sacred meal. Dangerously it crashed, it rolled over me, it broke behind me, but firm I stood and sought what I might see."

The Sun, Moon and Stars

According to their impact on diverse Native American cultures, the sun, moon and stars are assigned quite different personality traits. Thus, on the hot Plains, the sun is unquestionably male and predatory, while in the far north, where the spirit of the sun is shy and female, the moon is dominant and male. In Pawnee myth, the power of the sun spirit is tempered by the presence of the supreme creator, Tirawa. Another mythical creator, the Old Man of Blackfoot stories, is sometimes depicted as the sun's friendly rival.

In the mythic cosmogony of the Pawnee, all the celestial spirits ultimately owe their very existence and their powers to the Great Spirit, Tirawa. However, Tirawa arranged the sky spirits in such a way that there is a definite hierarchy. The most senior celestial spirit, after Tirawa, is the sun. This male sun spirit chased and seduced the spirit of the female moon, and their children, who rank immediately below them, are Great Star and Bright Star.

The "father" sun of Pawnee myth is identified as the provider both of game animals and of all the edible plants and fruits of the Earth. In one tale, the generous and protective father sun goes to the aid of a poor boy and his grandmother, providing the boy with a robe that has the power to create buffalo. As a result of his alliance with the sun, the orphan, who formerly was treated as an outcast, is able to provide game and wild vegetables for a starving village. In a different Pawnee tale, another orphan is similarly blessed by the sun with a magnificent, supernatural elk. The elk provides the orphan with meat and skin, after which it rises from Earth and re-enters the sun's disc from where it had originally come.

This 19th-century rawhide Sioux warrior's shield is decorated with the protective spirits of the sky. Even after the coming of guns, such shields were thought to offer spiritual protection.

The Triumph of the Sun

The Blackfeet of Montana tell a story which eloquently expresses the remorseless and invincible power of the sun. The creator, Old Man, was out hunting with this celestial body. The sun took

The Sun Snarer

In a story told by the Menomini people of Wisconsin, an unsympathetic sun is humbled by a resourceful young hunter. As he struggles to free himself from a magical, hair-spun snare, the mighty sun relies on the services of a puny mouse.

Two men went out to hunt in the forest, but refused to take their younger brother with them. Angry and upset to be left alone, and covering his body with his beaver-skin robe, the young boy lay down to weep. The morning sun rose, and at midday sent down a ray which shrank his robe and exposed the boy. "You have treated me cruelly and burned my robe," he shouted at the sun. "Why have you punished me? I do not deserve it!" The sun merely smiled and held its peace.

The boy gathered his burned robe and his bow and arrows and returned to the camp site. When his sister came into the tent and asked him why he was crying so bitterly, he told her of the sun's cruel treatment.

The next morning when the boy woke up, he said to her, "My sister, give me a thread!" She handed him sinew, but the boy returned it, saying, "No, I want a hair thread." So his sister plucked a hair from her head, and as the boy took the ends between his fingers, the hair began to lengthen. Then the boy returned to the place where he had first lain and, making a noose from his sister's hair, stretched it across the path. At the moment the sun touched it, the snare caught the sun around the neck and choked him. The cord was hot and became embedded in his neck. The sky grew dark and the sun cried out for his spirits to help him. He

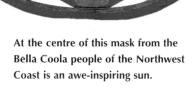

At the centre of this mask from the Bella Coola people of the Northwest Coast is an awe-inspiring sun.

implored a mouse to gnaw the thread, and after much labour, the mouse succeeded.

The boy then said to the sun: "For your cruelty I've punished you. You may go now." He returned to his sister, delighted with what he had done. And the sun rose once again and daylight returned.

down a bag from his sky home and pulled out a pair of embroidered leggings. "These are great medicine," he said. "All I have to do is put them on and walk around a patch of brush, and they set it on fire and drive out the deer for me to shoot."

Old Man determined to steal the leggings, and that night, when the sun had retired, he snatched them and made off. He travelled a long way and then lay down, using the leggings as a pillow. In the morning he woke to the sun's voice. "Old Man, what are you doing with my leggings under your head?" "Oh," replied Old Man, "I just needed a pillow, so I used your leggings!" The

next night, the same thing happened. Old Man ran till morning, but, fool that he was, he did not know that the whole world was the sun's domain. He could never hide from its all-seeing eyes.

The Sexing of the Sun

The Pawnee sun, and the sun of other Plains myths, is an unquestionably male character, while for the Inuit people of the Arctic the sun is a female and somewhat tragic persona. The Inuit spirit of the sun was originally a young woman. Abused by her brother, she mutilated herself in anger and grief, and then fled to the sky where she became *siqinim inua*, "the sun person". The Arctic sun, often spotted with molten-looking orange and red when it briefly appears in mid-winter, is identified by the Inuit as the sun sister rising up to display her terrible wounds. Although she only plays a relatively minor role in Inuit myth, she was, in Alaska, regarded as the provider of energy to children. Women who were nursing infants used to stand on the tops of their igloos on winter mornings and expose their children's legs to the rising sun. This was intended to let them absorb the sun's rays, so giving them strength and making them fast runners and good hunters.

The Arctic moon is prominent in long, clear winter nights so, unsurprisingly, it plays a prominent role in Inuit myth. Alingnaq, the guilty brother in the Inuit sun and moon myth, goes to the moon. There he lives in an immense igloo which he shares with the souls of the game animals. Caribou race around the inside walls of his lunar house. Outside, in an immense tub of sea water, Alingnaq keeps the souls of seals, whales and walruses. He has the power to give the bodies of these animals to humans. Alingnaq monitors people's behaviour closely. If they incur his displeasure, he withholds the animals on which

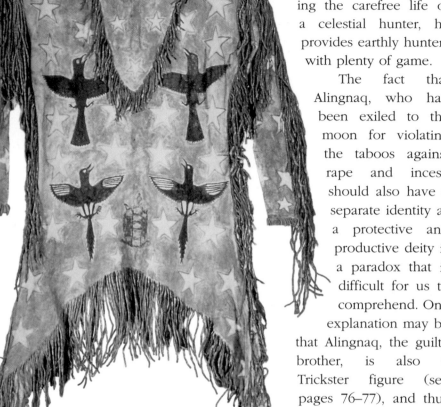

The stars, crows and magpies on this Arapaho Ghost Dance shirt, made *c*.1890, represent spirits of ancestors and natural forces, whose support the dancer enlisted in trying to bring order back to the spiritual cosmos (see page 130).

people's survival depends. At other times, as he wanders about the sky enjoying the carefree life of a celestial hunter, he provides earthly hunters with plenty of game.

The fact that Alingnaq, who had been exiled to the moon for violating the taboos against rape and incest, should also have a separate identity as a protective and productive deity is a paradox that is difficult for us to comprehend. One explanation may be that Alingnaq, the guilty brother, is also a Trickster figure (see pages 76–77), and thus is both a creative and a destructive being.

Other myths of the north see the moon as a benevolent force that comes to the aid of human beings. A story of the Gwich'in of Alaska describes how a poor boy, a shaman, who has magically provided his village with caribou, himself ascends to the moon. Before he disappears, he tells his mother: "I will go to the sky. There you will see me in the moon, holding a quarter of a caribou carcass. If there is going to be plenty of food on Earth, you will notice that I'm standing upright. But if there is going to be famine, I will be stooping over." The image of the destitute and outcast boy who is aided by a guardian spirit and then transported to the heavens is common to many Native myths about the celestial bodies.

The Boy Abducted by a Star

Not all relations between people and the spirits of the sky are happy. The Tsimshian people of the Northwest Coast have a story that shows how the sky spirits can on occasion be cruel.

One night a boy innocently talked to a star. "Poor fellow," he said, "you must be cold!" The star heard the boy's words, and came down to take him up to the sky. The boy's distraught parents searched everywhere for him. At last his father had news of his son. A woman who lived alone up a mountain said: "Your boy is tied to the smoke hole of the star man's house. He cries all the time. The sparks of the fire are burning his body." Then she told the man to make several arrows and shoot them into the sky until one stuck at the edge of the hole of the sky. The man did as she advised, and continued shooting until all of his arrows had stuck together, forming a line down to earth from the sky hole for him to climb up.

Once in the sky, the father fetched wood and carved some figures resembling his child. Then he made a fire and scorched the images to test them; eventually he found one made of yellow cedar that cried like a child. The man then travelled further in the sky until he came to the star man's house. The boy was, indeed, tied up near the edge of the smoke hole, and when the people inside stirred the fire in the house, the sparks made him cry. The father urged his son to be brave and bided his time.

When the father knew that the people in the house were sleeping, he untied the boy and put the yellow cedar image in his place. Then they ran off. In the morning, when the fire was going, the cedar image cried, but after a while it stopped. The star people realized what had happened and gave chase. But the father and son had reached the sky hole in time. They descended to earth on the chain of arrows, then pulled the arrows down after them. That was how the parents got back their son who had been stolen by the star man.

Spirits of Nature

Spirits of nature in Native American belief vary considerably in their power and significance. Some are seen as vast and even universal potencies, while others may hold sway over more specific aspects of the world, such as the wind, the sea, the rain or the animals. Still other spirits may be minor ghosts or sprites, appearing infrequently and only in restricted localities.

According to the Ojibway of the northwestern woodlands, when the Earth was made four major spirits were put in place for the benefit of humankind. These spirits lived in each of the four directions and also held up the corners of the heavens. The spirit of the north brought ice and snow, which helped people to track animal footprints. The spirit of the south provided the conditions that were favourable for the cultivation of pumpkins, melons, maize and tobacco. The western spirit was responsible for rain. And the spirit of the east brought light by commanding the sun to travel round the world.

This fragment of throat armour, made of shell by an ancient Mississippian artisan, is incised with crested woodpeckers, spiritual guardians of the four directions, and symbols of war.

Other Native American people also attributed spirits to the four cardinal points. The Iroquoian Wind Giant, Ga-oh, had four different animals – a bear, a panther, a moose and a fawn – at the mouth of his cave. When the north wind blew, the Iroquois said that the bear was at large in the sky. If the west wind blew, the panther was whining; the east wind was the moose "spreading his breath"; and the warm south wind was the "fawn returning to its doe".

Some spirits, such as the malevolent spirits of place that crop up in the landscape of the Alaskan Inuit, are best avoided. If resting travellers have mysteriously disappeared beside a certain rock, then future travellers will take care to make their camp at a safe distance from the evil spirit inhabiting that rock.

Other spirits are benign, such as those accorded elaborate honours on the occasion of the Green Corn dance, which was held every autumn by the northeastern Seneca. During the dance one of the prominent tribal elders would address the servants of the "master of life" who had sustained the people through the year. This long speech began with an expression of collective happiness "because we are still alive in this world". The thanksgiving continued: "Besides this act, we give thanks to the earth, and we give thanks also to all the things it contains. Moreover, we give thanks to the visible sky. We give thanks to the orb of light that daily goes on its course during the daytime. We give our thanks nightly also to the light orb that pursues its course during the night. So now we give thanks also to those persons, the Thunderers, who bring the rains. Also we give thanks to the servants of the Master of Life, who protect and watch over us day by day and night by night."

Sometimes, a thoughtless or selfish individual can offend a spirit of nature and affect everyone's welfare, but a spirit's wrath need not be experienced as a general, communal crisis. The nature

Spirits of the Seasons: Nipinouke and Pipounouke

The eternal cycle of the seasons that is repeated every year is described in this story of the Inuit as a partnership between two powerful spirits. The spirit Nipinouke brings spring and summer, while Pipounouke brings autumn and winter.

The spirits of the seasons are two beings known as Nipinouke and Pipounouke. These spirits divide the world between them, each keeping to his own side for as long as he can. But eventually the time comes when they have to change places.

When Nipinouke comes, he brings with him warmth, birds, green leaves and fresh grass. But as summer wanes, Nipinouke must give up his place.

Pipounouke then arrives, bringing autumnal decay and the winds, ice and snow of winter. He destroys all that Nipinouke created. In this way there is *Achitescatoueth*: succession in nature and balance in the world.

spirits, *kachinas* (see page 121), of southwestern Pueblo myths will remind individuals of their obligations towards the whole community. A Tewa story describes a day when everyone was told to gather onions. But two girls felt lazy and decided to do something else. Towards evening they thought better of their disobedience, and had just begun to gather onions when the sun started setting. Suddenly one of them heard a noise. A *kachina* spirit appeared. It held two long yucca blades. "You don't obey the chief," said the *kachina*, and drew out its whip. "We'll go with you!" cried the girls, assuming the *kachina* was a human being. "No, I did not come to bring you home," said the *kachina*, and started to whip them. The girls ran, followed by the spirit. As they ran, they scattered the onions; the laces of their moccasins broke; their leggings came off; their shawls and belts dropped to the ground. The *kachina* then said, "Don't do it again! When people go out, they should all go together. This is what happens to disobedient girls. Now go home." They went home without any onions, and without their moccasins, belts and shawls.

Native American communities were frequently conscious of a great multitude of invisible forces at work. The Inuit myth world provides a dramatic example of how various this spirit life

61

could be. In the Canadian Arctic, three major spirits ruled: the mother of the sea beasts, the moon spirit and the spirit of the air and weather. If a man spoke too assertively about his hunting skills, he risked offending the spirit of the air and weather, and bringing on a chastening blizzard. Similarly, if a woman violated taboo by preparing seal meat during her menstrual period, the offended mother of the sea beasts might withhold seals or walrus from the tribe.

Of primary importance to the hunters and fishers of the Arctic and the Northwest Coast were the spirits of living animals. Successful hunters did not simply slaughter their prey. Animals would ignore a hunter if he did not promise to acknowledge their spirits by offering them the appropriate death rites. Among the Alaskan Inuit, the whale's soul, which lay in its head, had to be returned to the sea with the head intact; otherwise the soul could not return to its place of origin and be reborn. Other large or significant animals, such as caribou and wolves, had to be ritually butchered to allow their spirits to escape from their lodgings in the neck. Provided that men and women performed these rites, the animals would help them by "lending their bodies" – that is, by allowing themselves to be hunted.

There was a multitude of other spirits: those of ancestors which dwelled near village graves and camp sites; spirits of place inhabiting lakes and rocks; and spirits invisibly roaming the air which might approach an individual who showed mystical susceptibility and make a shaman of him or her. Many traditional Native American belief systems attributed powerful spirits to animals, plants and other natural phenomena. One of the first native words learned by missionaries and explorers in the northeastern woodlands was the Algonquian term *manitou*, meaning "power, spirit, mystery" (see page 121). *Manitous* were simultaneously forces in their own right and spirits inhabiting animals, places, and the forces of nature. These powers were both helpful and vindictive. Even the shamans who controlled and interpreted spiritual forces were subject to their influence.

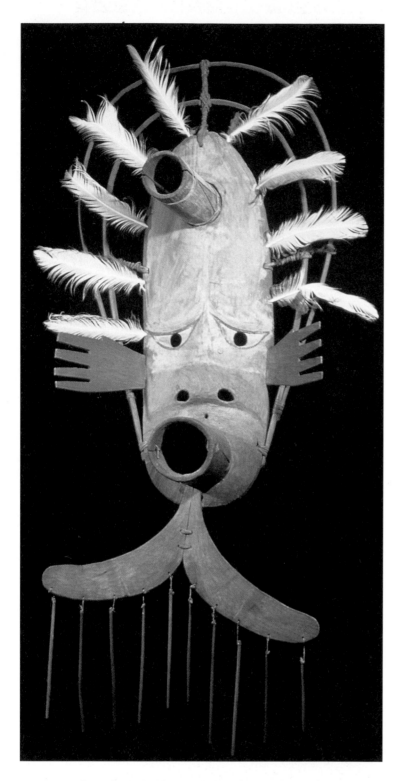

The Inuit wind-making spirit, Tomalik, is represented in this 19th-century shaman's mask. The winds of summer and winter blow through the tubes fitted in the mouth and forehead; white feathers evoke clouds and seabirds; and the lower pendants represent air bubbles rising from submerged seals.

The Corn Spirit

For a continuation of their blessings on hunting grounds and gardens, the spirits of nature had to be honoured. The northeastern Tuscarora people, as they harvested and stored their staple crop, acknowledged the spirit of corn.

In a village where the corn harvest had always been rich, people became lazy and careless. They forgot to weed and left corn to be trampled. They let the dogs eat the surplus and stored their seed in poorly dug holes and damaged baskets. Worst of all, they neglected to give proper thanks to the spirit of the corn.

Assuming that they could continue to get more food by hunting, the men roamed the forest for game. But the animals had vanished. The hungry people dug up their baskets. But their stores had rotted or been eaten by mice. Only one man, Dayohagwenda, had given thanks for his harvest and stored his corn securely.

Walking in the forest one day, Dayohagwenda came upon an elm bark lodge surrounded by weeds. Seated there was an old man. Dirty and ragged, the old man was weeping. "Grandfather, why do you weep?" asked Dayohagwenda. "Because your people have forgotten me," replied the elder. As Dayohagwenda pursued his questions, he realized that the old man was the spirit of the corn, and that he was dirty and ragged because the people had become careless and ungrateful. The spirit of corn was weeping because he thought that he had been forgotten.

Dayohagwenda returned to the village and found the people on the verge of starvation.

Recounting what he had seen, he warned that the spirit of the corn might leave them for ever. If, however, the people began honouring him again, the spirit would help them. Then Dayohagwenda dug up his own supplies and found that the spirit had increased them.

From that time on, the people honoured the spirit of the corn. They carefully planted, weeded, harvested and stored. And they always gave thanks to the spirit who blessed them.

This modern painting honours Selu, the first woman of Cherokee myth, who gave birth to corn after rubbing her stomach and produced the first beans from her breasts.

Thunder, Lightning, Fire, Rainbow

In many Native American traditions, unpredictable weather forces such as thunder, lightning and torrential rain are personified by the mythical Thunderbird. The more predictable properties of fire are encapsulated in origin myths that tell the story of a primal robbery. Often, as in stories about the theft of daylight, the intrepid fire-robbers are led by a Trickster animal.

The Thunderbird on this headdress is recognizable by his feathered horns and down-turned beak. The work of a Northwest Coast Kwakiutl artisan, the headdress was collected in 1926 and may date from the 19th century.

Great Man, the mythical creator of the Californian Maidu, made a world which originally was hot. The heat was so great that everything melted, and even today there is fire in stones and trees.

According to this conception, thunder is synonymous with Great Man. In other Maidu myths, however, lightning and thunder, though divine, are lesser deities bent on destroying humankind. This is the cue for the rainbow, which often appears at the end of storms, to come into view, and plead with the deities to have mercy on humans.

The rainbow is a benevolent spirit in almost all myths. To the Iroquoian Huron, it is a beautiful pathway on which various animals journey to the sky. In a Navajo story, Dawn Boy – a hero figure who aids human beings – ascends a rainbow to petition two powerful sky deities.

A myth of the Creek people of the Southeast describes how an orphan boy came upon two great beings, Tie-Snake and Thunder-being, wrestling by a river. Each combatant asked the boy to kill its adversary. Tie-Snake offered the boy knowledge, while Thunder-being promised him "all the thunder's power". The boy killed Tie-Snake. As a reward, he could always find game animals; in battle he was invulnerable; and he was able to use thunder and lightning to destroy his enemies.

Thunder is often an ambiguous being – feared and disliked, but capable of being outsmarted. In a story told by the Coeur d'Alene of Idaho, Thunder came to earth and stole a woman from her husband. The man set out in pursuit. At last, after a weary journey, he came to Thunder's house and found his wife inside. "You are dead. You are no longer a person," she said, "but let's dig a hole under the bed for you to hide in. In the meantime, I'll cook for Thunder. After dinner, he'll tell me stories. But when he falls asleep, we'll escape."

After some time, Thunder fell asleep and started to snore. The woman jumped up and dug out her husband. Picking up Thunder's shirts, she kept one and destroyed the rest. Then the couple ran to the edge of Thunder's mountain. The woman put on the shirt that she had taken from Thunder. They flew to Earth. She took off the shirt. "Be torn in pieces!" she cried and threw it away. Meanwhile, Thunder woke to find the woman gone. "There's no place I don't know. You are going to die," he said. He went to get his new shirt, only to find it gone. Defeated, he sat down and cried.

Mythical Fire-thieves

Almost always, fire is first brought to Earth for the benefit of humanity after a similar conflict. The starting point of most such fire-theft stories is that fire existed as a phenomenon in heaven before it reached Earth. Many fire-stealing stories describe how a team of animals climb a mountain that ascends high into the sky, and, sometimes in relay, make off with fire. In a tale of the southern Paiute, Coyote leads some birds on a fire-stealing mission. By pretending that they have come simply to gamble with their hosts, the fire-thieves trick their way into the fire-owners' realm. Coyote then makes off with some blazing cedar bark tied to his hair. When the fire-owners give chase, Coyote passes the fire first to the Crested Jay and then on to the other birds until they have outrun their pursuers. In order to demonstrate the fire-thieves' altruistic motive, Coyote finally announces: "Let's give heat and fire to all the trees and all the rocks!" Thus wood and stone, in the form of fire-drills, fire-wood and flints, have produced fire ever since.

Another fire-theft story, told by the Maidu, casts a being called Thunder as the fire-keeper. Fire has already appeared on earth and Thunder has stolen it; Earth's animals then set out to win it back. After Thunder has been tricked into parting with his fire, he enlists rain, wind and hail as quenchers of the fire-thieves' booty. Skunk, however, kills Thunder with an arrow, calling out, "Now you must stay up in the sky, and be the thunder." Thus it came about that fire remained on Earth and Thunder went to the sky.

Thunderbird

The fierce and sudden power of thunder is often represented as a huge eagle-like bird.

The Thunderbird is found in many Native American traditions. This immense mythical creature, whose wings make thunder and whose eyes and beak generate lightning, was primarily associated with the rain that brings fertility. Worshipped as a creator of new life, the Thunderbird was thought to inhabit craggy mountain peaks, from where it surveyed its vast hunting grounds. Among Northwest Coast peoples, it was believed to swoop down on the ocean to hunt whales, carrying them off in its talons and flying inland to devour them.

In many Plains cultures, the Thunderbird, which was known to the Lakota as Wakinyan, was regarded as a senior deity, second in rank only to Great Spirit. Images of the Thunderbird were frequently painted on shields, weapons, clothing and tents in order to inspire courage.

The Thunderbird is depicted on this 19th-century Clayoquot dance robe from the Northwest Coast.

The Society of Animals

The many animal characters that are found in Native American myths speak and behave in the same way as the humans whose existence depends on them. Often, the appearance and habits of a particular species, or clan, of animals derive from cosmic conflicts and other events. A common feature of all the stories is an assertion of the animals' spiritual power and importance.

Myths about the creation of Earth often begin with no people: the world's first inhabitants are the animals who bring about the conditions in which people can exist. Many creation stories describe a "dream time" in which humans and animals speak the same language and combine their skills to overcome obstacles or confront a mutual enemy (see pages 22–25). In such stories, different never means inferior; on the contrary, the animals of Native America are the spiritual equals of people.

While most stories about animals depict animal heroes (the mythical ancestors of such familiar creatures as coyotes, beavers and jays), there are also many stories that combine an account of the origins of certain animal families with explanations for their continuing behaviour. Thus, a story told by the Yana people of northern California about why and when the "geese people" first came to visit Mount Shasta also explains why geese continue to fly north in spring. Just as a traditional Yana headman might have sent a messenger to invite another village to a celebration, a mythical goose chief named Flint Rock sent Hummingbird to invite the crane, geese and heron people to a dance celebration: "Wrapping a wildcat skin about his head, Hummingbird made himself ready and flew south to summon the geese people … Very pretty was Meadow Lark Woman with her apron of rodent bones strung on buckskin tassels."

To reach the dance hosted by Flint Rock, the mythical geese people took their bearings and flew in formation, just as real geese do now: "All the geese people, every sort of person that was there, had wings. The geese people filed up from the south, dancing as they went north. They flew up into the air, and continued their dance northwards while flying."

A creation story of the Californian Karok describes the first animals as "all alike in power. No one knew which animals should be food for others." The creator, Kareya, ordained that Man should give the animals their rank. Kareya told Man to make bows and arrows and to give them to each animal. The longest bow would go to the animal which was to have the greatest power, the shortest to the one which

A 19th-century Tsimshian raven rattle. This raven-human-raven carving illustrates the fusion of animal and human identities in the myths of the Northwest Coast.

How the Mohawk Rabbit Dance Began

The animals of Native American myths and folktales often live in clan-like groups, under the guidance of an especially wise or experienced chief, or "master". In this tale a master rabbit initiates a ritual that is observed for ever after by the Mohawk.

A group of hunters was once travelling through the forest when they came to a clearing. As the leader approached the glade, he saw a creature.

The animal was the size of a small black bear, but it was not a bear. In fact it was an enormous rabbit. As the men watched, the rabbit raised its head. But instead of fleeing, it nodded toward the men and thumped the earth with one of its back feet. At this signal, crowds of other rabbits joined the big rabbit. Now the big rabbit started thumping rhythmically, as though beating a drum. The rabbits formed a circle and danced around the rabbit drummer. Suddenly the master rabbit was still. The drumming stopped. He leapt into the air, then vanished into the forest.

When the hunters returned to the village, they went to the longhouse and described what they had seen. "Beat the rhythm of the rabbit chief," said one of the elders. The men took their drums, and the people began dancing to the rhythm set by the rabbit chief. This rabbit dance was their repayment to the animals whose meat and skins they made so much use of.

was to have the least. The animals then met and went to sleep, awaiting Man's arrival. When the sun rose next day, Man gave the longest bows to Mountain Lion and Bear and the shortest to Frog. Coyote, who had slept through the ceremony, received no bow at all. Instead he was awarded cunning, and "therefore was friendly to Man" in the future.

Many animal stories are spun out into long sagas concerning epic quests undertaken by different species; the animals' journeys often represent the wandering of tribal ancestors. Other animal tales, however, are extremely short. The Inuit tell stories, often accompanying a game of cat's cradle, that may last no longer than a few seconds; for example: "A lemming circled the skylight of an igloo. Suddenly it fell, shouting, 'I think I've broken my ribs!'" Tales like these, which are often sung with the addition of nonsensical choruses, are simply enjoyed as entertainment. In contrast, some short tales are instructive, such as the sad story of the quail family that is related by the Pima of Arizona: "A mother quail had twenty children and wandered the country in search of water. At last they found a foul, muddy pond. They were all so thirsty that they drank the water. The water was so bad it killed them." The moral of this myth is simply that the quails died because they did not know, as they should have known, how to recognize healthy water.

Animal Souls and the Afterlife

Animals were obviously important for the traditional lifestyles of Native America. Their flesh was human meat, their skin human clothes, their bones and sinews made weapons and tools. But their material importance was matched by their no less obvious spiritual value. To continue to hunt, hunters had to pay due reverence to the souls of the hunted.

In Native American myth, animals are regarded as holy because they have powerful souls. And though the souls of some species, such as bears, whales and elk, may be greater, more important or more dangerous to humans than those of, say, squirrels and lemmings, all animals share an honourable status in the spiritual universe.

Animals were present in the ancient dream time, when every being and every thing participated in sacred newness. Their presence, "back then", is a guarantee of their holiness, but in traditional practice, as well as mythical stories, animals are always treated with respect. When hunting was widespread most Native American hunters justified their actions with the belief that the immortal souls of their prey would return to their villages for reincarnation. If people killed and butchered an animal "kindly" – by using sharp, clean weapons and following rituals which would please both the individual and its species – then the animal's soul would not resent its "death". When the soul reached its homeland, it would report the hunter's behaviour. If the hunter had done everything correctly, the soul might say: "I will return in my new life to that man. He and his wife are good and generous people. They

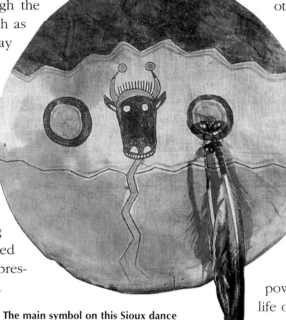

The main symbol on this Sioux dance shield is a buffalo. Such symbols acted as talismans that invoked the power and courage of an esteemed animal.

share what they hunt. They cut my body with skill and respect. You others can go to that hunter too."

If the hunter was slovenly, lazy or disrespectful, then the animal spirit might refuse to come again to him, and would warn the souls of the entire species to avoid him as well. Withdrawal was only one way of punishing a miscreant human: the animals had other ways of showing their displeasure. In particular they could use their soul power to endanger the hunter's life or cause him to fall ill.

Perhaps the most feared and honoured of all animal souls was that of the bear. Among the Kwakiutl of the Northwest Coast, a hunter who had killed a grizzly bear took on its power, the man's soul becoming imbued with that of the animal. The following speech of a successful Kwakiutl hunter on meeting a bear demonstrates how such animals were regarded. "Be ready friend, that we may try our strength. You dreaded one! ... Listen to me, Supernatural One, now I will take by war your power of not respecting anything, of not being afraid, and your wildness, great, good, Supernatural One." Here the man acknowledges the supernatural status of the bear while also declaring himself the bear's equal in strength by virtue of his own previous victorious encounters.

Guardian Spirits

The souls of animals could also be enlisted by people as their guardian spirits. In many communities, animal souls were sought out by apprentice shamans and young men and women undergoing initiation rites at puberty. The Algonquin, for example, sought an animal *manitou* or "spirit" (see page 121); the Inuit sought a *tuunraq* ("helping spirit"). Among the Tlingit of southeast Alaska a young man might take a river otter, cut out its tongue and hang this round his neck. The spirit of the otter residing in the tongue was thought to provide the owner with an understanding of the language spoken by all animals.

The spirits of animals could also be invoked for the purpose of healing or self-transformation. Shamans wore the skins, tails, claws and heads of animals that they had encountered in their vision quests. In administering to a sick person, a shaman would dance, shaking all his animal amulets to invoke the souls that they represented, and would then proceed to call upon one or more animal spirits to restore the patient's health. The mutually binding relationship between the shaman and the animal meant that the spirit could be persuaded to exert a supernatural curative power. In another reflection of a guardian spirit's influence, the shaman could use an amulet to transform himself temporarily into the shape of the animal itself, and call upon its spiritual power in this way.

The afterlife of animals was generally perceived as being happy. Dead animals lived in soul-villages and they ranged over extensive plains resembling those they had enjoyed in their earthly existence (see page 124). Native Americans believed that the souls of buffalo continued to graze on the plains of the afterlife long after their real numbers on the Great Plains had been reduced to a few isolated herds by the white men's depredations in the 1880s. In some cultures, fearsome animals guarded the river leading to the other world. The Ojibway people of the Great Lakes maintained that a huge serpent served as a bridge spanning this river. This was benign enough to other animals; but threatened to devour

shamans in search of spirit helpers. Animals also inhabited the world of the human afterlife. The souls of dogs would often pass down the same road as human souls and would continue to be devoted to their masters; the other animals provided game for human souls who coursed the "happy hunting grounds". The Great Hare, who was the deity and culture hero of the Algonquian people of the Northeast, also presided over the next world.

However, by no means all of the animal souls encountered in the afterlife were friendly. The Iroquois believed that a ferocious dog stood at the far end of the bridge leading to the land of the dead. Similarly, the Senel people of California thought that a dangerous buffalo bull stood in the path of the soul of every deceased person. Those people who had led a good life were allowed to pass by, but those who had behaved wickedly fell victim to this menacing creature.

Salmon had more than a simple nutritional significance for the peoples of the Northwest Coast. The annual salmon runs were a constant reminder of the cyclical flow of life and death, and salmon were perceived as humans in another form. Every year, the underwater salmon people exchanged their human clothes for those of fish and migrated upstream to be fished by humans. After they had been eaten, their bones floated back to the sea, where, once again, they would become salmon people. This wooden Tlingit sculpture, collected in 1898, represents the living human aspect of the salmon's identity.

Soul Theory and Spirit Flight

Within the Native American cosmos there is no separation between the spiritual and material, between the natural and the human, between life and death, or between body and soul. Any single body is likely to house a variety of spirits or souls – one that emerges during dreams or sickness, one that dies with the body, one that joins the afterlife, and one that manifests itself as a delinquent ghost.

The Native American cosmos is populated not just by the living, but also by countless souls; these are invoked and propitiated in countless myths and rituals. Shamans, or "holy people", were masters of the art of soul exchange and soul flight. Usually, though not invariably, these holy people were adult men, who became "soul doctors" only after intense solitary experiences that proved their ability to tame or at least direct the power of souls. An apprentice shaman would retreat to some lonely, spirit-receptive place, where, after a period of fasting, he would endure a psychic struggle with an aggressive, invasive spirit. In their subsequent soul flights, qualified shamans, aided by drumming, dancing and singing, could fly to other spheres to encounter the spirit of the moon or sun, or plunge to the sea bed to meet the spirits of the ocean.

However, the mobile spirits of traditional Native American belief were not always benign. Bad spirits could enter an individual and cause mental illness, often diagnosed as temporary soul loss. In such cases, a shaman's expertise was required. On a soul flight, the shaman would journey to where the patient's soul had been taken. There, he would wrestle with whatever malign spirit had abducted the soul and, if successful, guide the missing spirit home.

Animal spirits sometimes help deserving people, but they may afterwards want to keep them in their spirit houses. A story of the Northwest Coast Bella Coola people describes how a man called Kuna was helped by mouse spirits, yet still managed to return to his family. Kuna had married into another tribe, and used to go hunting with his brothers-in-law. Whenever he shot at sea lions, the brothers would object to his bowmanship. One day, they decided to get rid of him. One of the hunters pretended that he had lost his whetstone and, when Kuna was sent back for it, the rest of the hunting party deserted him. Kuna sat down and cried. Presently he fell asleep, but was woken by a voice saying: "I invite you to my chief's house." Kuna looked around but, seeing no one, went back to sleep. This happened again, but the third time Kuna looked, he saw a mouse. "Don't hide, supernatural one," said Kuna, "I see you now." Kuna followed the mouse to the mouse chief's house. "Go kill a dog, so that Kuna may eat," said the mouse chief to his followers. While Kuna waited, an old woman came up. "Take this basket," she said. "When they give you meat, do not eat it, but put it in the basket, or you will never return home. Long ago I ate the spirits' meat and so I cannot return." Then the meat was brought, and while the mouse chief ate, Kuna did as he had been told. The spirits realized that he had not eaten and prepared to return him. They fetched a skin-bag and put him inside it. "When you hear a bird settle on the bag," they said, "snap your fingers. The bird and the winds will guide you ashore." They floated Kuna on the water, and the south and west winds blew him homeward. Before long he had reached his wife's village. When his children saw him they ran to tell their mother. "Your father is dead," she said. But soon they realized that he had returned alive, saved by the spirits.

The soul of a salmon is evoked by this Inuit shaman's mask from southeast Alaska. The seven pendants are stylized representations of the fish shape, designed to reinforce the mask's magic powers.

The Next Life

In the mythologies of Native America death has no dominion. Life on earth is followed by a spiritual existence in another realm, the afterlife. Sometimes this is visualized as a blissful, heaven-like continuation of earthly life; at other times, it is pictured as being more like hell. Many stories describe people who briefly cross over into the afterlife, mingle with the spirits who are assembled there, and then come back to resume their life on earth after their experience.

Life after death, according to the traditions of southwestern Hopi, Zuni and Tewa peoples, is an extension of life on earth. The dead journey to what is often an underground or underwater village, where they join the spirits of people they were associated with in life. Some of these spirits of the dead might once have specialized as hunters, athletes, shamans or dancers; or they might have been rainmakers who now have the form of clouds and lightning. Benevolent ancestral spirits, the *kachinas*, keep company with the souls of humans in this subterranean territory, and invite certain human souls to come as guests to a *kachina* dance house, or to *Wenima*, a beautifully wooded and watered afterlife resort.

The afterlife of Pueblo belief seldom involves any strict separation, familiar from Christian ideas of the Last Judgment, between saved and lost souls, but the Hopi tradition does contain the notion of punishment after death. On the path to the place where the Hopi emerged onto Earth (*sipapu*) in the Grand Canyon (*Oraibi*), the "breath body" of the deceased traveller is met by a guardian called Tokonaka. If Tokonaka judges the traveller to be good, he lets him or her proceed to the town of the dead. Otherwise, a spirit traveller might have to journey on a forked trail leading to a series of up to four fire pits. If the spirit can be purified in the first pit, it can return to the trail of the good. The incorrigibly evil are burnt in the fourth fire pit.

The possibility that "dead" souls, at some unspecified but favourable time, can be reborn on Earth arises in many Native American afterlife traditions. Thus one Inuit view is that the Raven Man

This Hopi *kachina* figure, made in 1939 by William Quotskuyva, represents Masau'u, the protector of the living and ruler of the dead. His role as lord of the underworld is expressed by the goggle eyes and protruding teeth of his skull-like mask.

hero who, at the beginning of time, perfected the creation, will return after a universal holocaust with the souls of the dead and re-establish life in its primal goodness. Smohalla, the holy man who inspired the nineteenth-century Dreamers Cult of the Northwest Coast, declared: "I want my people to stay with me here. All the dead men will come to life again. Their spirits will come to their bodies again. We must wait here in the homes of our fathers and be ready to meet them in the bosom of the mother." A generation later, Smohalla's vision was echoed and amplified by Wovoka, the prophet of the Ghost Dance Movement of the Plains (see page 130). In their struggle against the white men, the Dreamers and the Ghost Dancers enlisted the help of the sacred spirits of their ancestors, of the buffalo and of the elements. With the aid of these spirit powers, they hoped to bring about a return of the old ways and a restoration of cosmic harmony.

The Ghost House

Though death was not terminal and therefore not to be feared, ghosts were often objects of horror. This Tsimshian story from the Northwest Coast features a frightening Ghost chief.

Brown Eagle, a chief's son, ate only salmon. When he grew up, he became sick and died. His grieving parents put salmon on his grave, and the village moved to a new site. After two years, some young women and young men went to dig fern roots at the old site. At supper, they sat down to a meal of salmon. One foolish boy cried, "Look, this is Brown Eagle's food!" Everyone laughed, and one of them said, "Let's see if he'll come from his grave when we call him. We can feed him salmon." One of the men promptly took the fish and offered it at Brown Eagle's grave. In vain, the women implored them not to mock the dead. Suddenly a frightful noise was heard from the graveyard. Brown Eagle's skeleton was approaching with arms outstretched. "Let me have it!" he roared. Everyone was terrified. Some fell into the fire. Others tried to escape, but the ghost took their breath away. When the village discovered what had happened, they consulted their shamans. One of them said, "The souls of our young are now living in the Ghost Chief's house. If we claim our youths tonight, they could return!" The shaman told his colleagues to shake their rattles and amulets. "The Ghost House shamans will answer. Then the ghosts will run out and each of us can take the soul of a young

This Tlingit rattle in the form of a salmon with a shaman rider vividly illustrates the holy man's capacity to harness the spirit power of animals.

person." When they shook their rattles, the Ghost House shamans replied. The village shamans rushed into the house and grabbed the people's souls. They restored them to the bodies they belonged to, and gradually purged the ghostly air that hung over the young people.

73

KEEPERS OF ORDER

An Indian family is canoeing downstream early one evening, travelling from their spring hunting grounds to one of their summer campsites. The group consists of three generations – old people, young adults and children. From time to time, the young adults seek advice from the elders, who respond quietly, gesturing towards the river, the woods and the mountains. Sometimes they reply tersely, while on other occasions they begin to relate stories. The tales they tell are about places they have been to, adventures of their tribal forebears, animals they have hunted, and their spirit visions.

Such conversations were a constant feature of Native American life. They always took a similar form, irrespective of whether they took place among the Sioux or the Huron, the Kwakiutl or the Zuni. Discussion would centre on local knowledge about the land, seasonal changes, animal behaviour and where useful plants might be found. The older people who were well versed in such wisdom were held in high esteem by their community, for without their knowledge the group could not operate efficiently. Yet the elders' ancestors, long since dead, had an even higher status. Most societies had a fund of memories of recent ancestors; the further back these memories went, the grander and more heroic the stories and their central characters became.

Tales narrated by the tribal elders thus performed several functions: they taught the younger generations how to hunt, travel and survive, but also anchored the present firmly in past experience. A sense of place and history was essential to Native American society, and mythology was regarded as just another form of history, albeit from a pre-tribal era. The major events that had occurred in the time before human memory were conveyed to each generation in the form of myths about the Tricksters, heroes and monsters of prehistory. Although these figures were seen as inhabiting a supernatural realm, the results of their actions were clearly evident in the present day in such topographic features as hills, lakes and canyons. The tangible signs of myth therefore had as great a significance as the accomplishments of recent forebears. However inhospitable the terrain or difficult the hunting, each tribe came to terms with its environment by peopling it with figures from both the real and the mythological past.

Left: **An Indian encampment on the shore of Two Medicine Lake in Montana.**

Below: **A model of a canoe, made by the artist Tomah Joseph (1837–1914) from the Passamaquoddy Indian Reservation in Maine.**

75

Tricksters: The Unpredictable Spirits

The Trickster – a mischievous and capricious figure who deceives and exploits his fellow creatures for his own gratification – is found in the stories of all Native American peoples. He commonly appears as a semi-divine but largely amoral presence at the creation of the world. In the guise of Raven, Coyote or Hare, a Trickster may permanently transform such natural phenomena as an animal's appearance or the course of a river. But as often as he tricks others, a Trickster is himself duped and humbled. And however selfish and coarse he is, a Trickster's antics provoke affectionate laughter, while his mythic power inspires awe.

The generic term "Trickster" is an invention of European and white American writers, and wherever a Trickster figure appears in Native American myths, he was known only by his local name. Stories abound of Tricksters in the form of a Coyote, Raven or Hare, particularly among the Plains Indians and the peoples of the Southwest and Northwest Coast. But Tricksters also appear in human or semi-human form. Among the Ojibway and Menomini, the Trickster was essentially the same being as the hero Manabozho (see pages 82–83). And in Alaskan Inuit myth, the Moon Spirit who deceived his sister and then became master of the game animals was also a Trickster (see page 58).

Among the most famous series of Trickster stories was that related by the Siouan-speaking Winnebago of central Wisconsin. In these tales, a tribal chief breaks religious and sexual taboos and then goes on the warpath. Talking nonsense and renouncing his social status, the ex-chief is shunned as a wicked person. He then embarks on a solitary journey, "calling all the objects in the world younger brothers" and speaking to them in their own tongues. At this point, the chief becomes a Trickster, and a series of loosely connected tales relates how he roams the world, sometimes transforming things for the good, but mostly interfering mischievously in the affairs of animals and people. The exploits of this "Older Brother," as some creatures call him, are variously feared, marvelled at or viewed with indulgence and humour by his fellow beings. The Trickster himself is regarded by turns as cunning, intelligent, foolish or unlucky.

These contrasting character traits emerge clearly from two stories told by the Ojibway about the Trickster and wonder-worker Manabozho. In the first, his skilful subterfuge brings him success in hunting. One day, Manabozho enticed a lone moose by claiming to be its estranged brother. As the animal drew near, Manabozho asked it whether it had heard the news about the person who killed his brother. Not realizing that the Trickster was alluding to its own impending death, the moose was caught off guard, even letting itself be persuaded to stand with its head averted, at which point Manabozho promptly shot it.

The other side of Manabozho's character emerges from a story relating how he once fell asleep, having ordered his rear end to guard some fowl roasting on a fire. When the birds were stolen and no alarm raised, the Trickster foolishly set his own hind quarters alight as punishment.

Many animal spirits are depicted on this Kwakiutl cedarwood totem pole. One of the principal Native American Trickster figures, the Raven, is second from the base.

A Foolish Dive

Many stories show the Trickster as a victim of his own false perceptions. In this Arapaho legend, a figure called Nihansan dives into water to gather fruit that are merely reflections.

One day, Nihansan was walking by a stream when he spotted some juicy red plums under the water. He desperately wanted to eat them, so he undressed, dived into the water and groped about on the stream bed, trying to collect the fruit.

He emerged from the stream empty-handed, but resolved to try again. Taking some stones, he tied them to his wrists and ankles to weigh himself down under water. He plunged in for a second time, and searched the bottom in vain. Eventually, when he could hold his breath no longer, he released the stones and floated up to the surface.

Looking up, he suddenly noticed plums hanging on a tree above him. "You fool!" he said to himself, and climbed out of the water. He went to the tree, where he ate some of the plums and picked some more for his onward journey.

Many Ojibway stories about Manabozho portray him on the move in search of fun and gratification. Yet however dissolute and wilful he allows himself to be, his transforming power is always present. One story recounts how he persuaded a group of swans, geese and ducks to dance for him with their eyes closed. Beating his drum with one hand, he broke the necks of these water fowl with the other. Only the "Hell-diver" (loon) opened its eyes and escaped, for which Manabozho punished the bird by giving it its characteristic red eyes.

Several Winnebago stories end with the Trickster undergoing a character change and becoming a transformer after a series of mishaps. In one such tale, the Trickster is weary of life on Earth. He suddenly recalls why Earthmaker sent him to the world. As a last sign of his nobler disposition, he travels round removing hindrances to humans, for example by altering the course of rivers and clearing mountain passes of obstacles. Then he retires to heaven, leaving Hare in charge of the Earth.

Raven and Hare

The Raven was a highly important Trickster figure in the myths of many Native cultures. For peoples of the Northwest Coast, the Arctic and the Subarctic, Raven was, and still is, a heroic creator. Elsewhere, other figures such as Hare filled the Trickster role.

Countless Native American myths describe how Raven created the world, yet also treat him as the supreme Trickster. This seeming paradox may ultimately derive from conflicting attitudes towards the real bird – for example, the Koyukon Indians of central Alaska regard ravens as clever birds, but also consider their behaviour unpredictable and comic. Moreover, while ravens appear quick-witted and keenly aware of human behaviour, they are actually lazy scavengers, living off the food that animals and people have made efforts to hunt.

As a creator, Raven made the world twice over. The first world was a paradise: meat was plentiful, and rivers flowed in both directions, so people never had to paddle their canoes. But Raven thought this world too easy for humans, and so remade it in its familiar form, with all its hardships and woes. This primal Great Raven is revered among Northwest Coast peoples as the "grandfather" figure to whom people attribute creative

and healing power and to whom they pray for luck in hunting, good health and prosperity.

Yet Raven has a negative dimension to his character, which emerges in his reputation for selfishness and greed. Both real ravens and the Raven Trickster are thought to lead an easy life, and some contempt attaches to them accordingly. Myths describe Dotson'sa (the Great Raven creator) as sleeping in dog-skin blankets, whose foul smell and roughness were repellent to people.

The paradox of Raven's character, and of the ambivalent attitudes shown towards him, is expressed in a multitude of myths and legends from the Northwest Coast. To peoples of this region, Raven is a creator and transformer, but also a buffoon and dupe. The Haida call him Power-of-the-Shining-Heavens, as he made both day and night. Likewise, he created the great rivers, the forests that teem with wildlife, the useful trees and berries and the sea with all its fish and mammals.

Alongside accounts of these achievements are comic tales of Raven's mischief-making and humiliation. In a story told by the Nootka of British Columbia, some old people were sitting watching a woman with eight braids of hair who was walking on the beach. She carried with her a stick,

A 19th-century Tlingit emblem hat, worn for ceremonial occasions by members of the Raven clan. Throughout North America, the Raven was a widespread Trickster hero, held responsible for bringing light to earth.

**The Trickster figure Hare is shown in this Navajo weaving.
Hare is both a benefactor and a clown, and, like
other Tricksters, can effect transformations.**

and began to dig up clams. Soon a tall figure with black hair appeared. The people recognized the pair as Octopus and Raven, and knew that Raven would begin to pester Octopus.

Raven duly sat down on a rock and asked her, "Octopus, are you digging for clams?" Octopus woman continued to dig in silence. Raven repeated his question, but still got no reply. Suddenly, after he had asked for a fourth time, Octopus's braids turned into tentacles. Wrapping four around Raven and four around the rock, she said, "Raven, I'm glad you asked that question. Yes. I am digging clams. These are clams. And I am digging them." Raven struggled. The tide was coming in. "You have answered my question,

Octopus. Thank you. Now please let me go." But, as the water became deeper, Octopus kept repeating her answer and held Raven fast. The water rose over his head, and the people saw him drown. They were unconcerned, however, as they knew he would come to life again. And indeed, the very next day, Raven was back. But he refrained from asking Octopus any more questions.

Hare is another Trickster figure in Native mythology. In stories of the Winnebago, he is born of a virgin who dies, leaving him in the care of his grandmother. As Hare roams the world, he acts as both benefactor and clown. His grandmother, who represents the spirit of the Earth, often has to rescue him or excuse his mistakes.

Coyote, a Sly Wild Dog

Native American mythology has more stories about Coyote as a Trickster than about any other animal or character. This may derive from the fact that the coyote thrives throughout almost all of North America. Many creation myths show the half-animal, half-human Coyote as playing a major role in the early days of the Earth.

Like the raven – its counterpart in Trickster stories – the real coyote is a scavenger, yet it also hunts for itself, taking small rodents and rabbits and cleverly concealing its uneaten food. Many Coyote myths reflect both admiration and contempt for this resourceful beast. On the one hand, Coyote is a hero who helps organize the primordial world. On the other, he is the buffoon whose adventures resemble those of Raven and other Tricksters such as Manabozho (see pages 76–77). Some stories, such as those of the Caddo of the Southeast, also show Coyote starting his career as hero and transformer, and then changing into a Trickster, or even an evil character.

This 18th-century carved adze handle from the Chinook culture of the Northwest Coast has twin images of the Trickster Coyote perched on the shoulders of a spirit helper. Coyote appears in the creation myths of many Native American peoples.

In the beginning, according to the Caddo, the Great-Father-Above created the physical world, but it was Coyote who helped people organize their society. As the early physical and social world developed, certain things needed altering. The sun, for example, travelled too fast. So Coyote decided to intervene. He went to meet the sun, and accompanied it on its westward journey. After engaging it in casual conversation, Coyote went into the bushes on the pretext of relieving himself and asked the sun to wait. But Coyote never returned, and even though the sun eventually gave up waiting and resumed its journey, it could not make up lost time. In this way, Coyote extended the hours of daylight.

Despite bringing such benefits to humanity, however, Coyote was usually depicted as thoroughly bad. The final episode of the Caddo sun story tells how the Great-Father-Above threatened to banish Coyote for his mean tricks. Although Coyote repeatedly promises to desist, he cannot overcome his Trickster nature, and so is exiled. Many other tales about Coyote end in his exclusion from society, or even his death. Yet he is indestructible, always springing back to life to embark upon new adventures.

A sandpainting by the Navajo of the Southwest depicts several creator beings, among whom are the First Man, First Woman and Coyote.

Coyote and Bear

Tricksters often come into conflict with other creatures. In this story, told among the Northern Paiute, Coyote emerges victorious from a feud with Bear. However, even in cases where the Trickster figure is killed, he is always able to regenerate himself.

Coyote once exacted revenge on Bear, who had killed and eaten his son. He finally tracked Bear down beside a stream, where he was dozing after a meal of berries. Coyote hid and called out, "What are you hunting?" "Berries and chokecherries," said the Bear. "Did you ever do mischief?" "No," replied Bear. But Coyote prompted the Bear into recalling that he had eaten a child about a year before. Coyote resolved to trick him. "You'll find lots of berries on that hill over there," he called. "You might think someone wants to shoot you, but don't be alarmed." As soon as Bear had climbed the hill, Coyote shot him, lit a fire and roasted him. As the meat was cooking, he began to play with some split trees that the wind was opening and closing, but got his hand stuck. While he was incapacitated, some crows came and ate the bear meat. Coyote eventually freed himself and ate the bone marrow. Piling up the bones, he sang: "I'm a pretty strong person. Even if you kill me, I'll come back to life. Even if the grass is growing through my bones."

A Plains Indian shield depicting the figure of a bear, an animal widely respected for its great strength.

Another story told by the Caddo describes how Coyote was distracted from hunting buffalo by a turkey roosting in a tall tree. He called to the bird: "If you don't come here, I'll climb the tree. If you fly to another, I'll break it down and kill you. Only if you fly towards the prairie will you be safe. I have no power over anything on the prairie." The turkey unwisely took Coyote at his word and made for the prairie, where the Trickster easily ran it down, killed it and began to devour it. Glancing slyly about him as he ate to see if anyone was watching, Coyote thought he caught a glimpse out of the corner of his eye of someone standing behind him ready to strike. Without waiting to see who it was, he called on a skill he had been endowed with since the beginning of time, and began to run. He ran ever faster, but could not elude his pursuer. Eventually, he gave up and rolled over on his back to beg for mercy. But as he did so, he heard something crack. This turned out to be a turkey feather that had lodged between two of his upper teeth and, sticking up vertically just behind his right eye, had deceived him into thinking he was being followed. When he realized that he had been fooled by a mere feather, Coyote was furious. Ever since that time, according to the story, the coyote has had a wild appearance, loping away slowly at first and constantly glancing to his right to see if he is being followed.

Heroes of Myth and History

Heroes of Indian mythology were almost always male, and were often the product of a miraculous birth. Straddling the world of spirits and humans, they were ambiguous characters. In addition, historical figures were often accorded legendary status.

The hero Trickster Manabozho was the product of a union between a human being and a spirit. The story of his birth is told in a legend of the Menomini of the Lake Michigan region. At the beginning of time there lived an old woman with a single daughter. Every day the woman left her daughter in their tent and went to dig potatoes. But the young woman hated being left alone and finally persuaded her mother to let her accompany her. The old woman gave her a hoe, on one strict condition: that she faced south as she laboured and never turned round. The two women worked for a while, but, distracted by conversation and the pleasure she took in her new occupation, the young woman did indeed turn round. No sooner had she done so than she was swept off her feet by a great wind and blown into some nearby bushes. As the mother had feared, her daughter had attracted, and been impregnated by, the male north wind. The result of this union was Manabozho, who was raised by his grandmother after his mother died in childbirth.

Many hero stories start with such magical impregnations. But heroes may also be the supernaturally born "grandchildren" of solitary old women. Northwest Coast people often describe the Trickster Raven – part human, part bird – as the grandchild and companion of the "earth crone", or primal grandmother, who is believed to have existed from the beginning of time. Once created, one of Raven's exploits is to engineer his

A Haida mask depicting the figure of Raven. Masks such as this would be worn for dance performances that took place during ceremonial rituals.

own supernatural rebirth. One account describes how Raven wishes to enter the household of the people who are hoarding daylight. To gain entrance, he transforms himself into a pine needle and drops into a cup of water. When the daughter of the family drinks from the cup, the pine needle miraculously makes her pregnant. After Raven is duly reborn as a human, he can proceed with his planned theft of the light.

Many Native American mythical heroes have a complex character. The hero is a human being, whose life on earth is just like that of legendary early people. But he is touched with divine power, which makes him physically gigantic, enormously powerful and capable of overcoming the strongest of enemies. Moreover, the hero may share some characteristics with the Trickster. In the story above, Raven is a hero because he brought light to Earth, but he achieves this through deceit.

As a semi-divine human, the hero may often have to rid the world of monsters and dangerous spirits. Yet in his guise as Trickster, he frequently resorts to subterfuge and violence, irrespective of circumstances. One famous episode from Manabozho's life illustrates these dual characteristics. Manabozho once learned of a forthcoming game of lacrosse between the

deities of the sky and the underworld, to take place on a huge site across an area stretching from present-day Detroit to Chicago. On the morning of the game, he turned himself into a great pine tree so that he could watch the game unnoticed. The contest began amid much noise and inconclusive skirmishing. But as the game went on, Manabozho became so engrossed in the action that he changed back into a man and began shooting arrows at the underworld gods. Enraged, they chased Manabozho, who narrowly escaped by climbing to the top of a tall tree. As the Trickster turned victim, Manabozho's plan misfires. Yet it is in his role as a hero that he intervenes in the contest in the first place, for the benefit of humanity.

Orphan Heroes

At the outset of their adventures, many of the heroes of Native American cultures are on the margins of society. Several Alaskan Inuit narratives describe how a destitute boy, sometimes accompanied by his grandmother, gains social status or becomes a shaman by displaying intelligence or bravery. These heroic figures may then be called upon to rid the world of such destructive entities as giant rodents or dangerous women who practise shamanistic rites. Most of the tales end with the death of the animals and the socialization of the women through marriage and childbirth.

Further stories from Inuit cultures describe how orphans undertake supernatural quests. These ordeals usually involve outwitting hostile spirits. The hero of an Alaskan story, a young adventurer called Ukunniq, is so poor that he has holes in his boots. His first encounter is with spirits who have devised a deadly game for him, involving splitting a log with potentially lethal whalebone wedges. Protected by a magical amulet, Ukunniq terrifies the spirits by threatening them – semi-humorously – with the toes that protrude through his boots. The serious message of the story is that the boy derives his shamanistic power from his poverty. He grows in stature

This painting of a Medicine Mask Dance (1850), by the Canadian
artist Paul Kane, shows masked Klallam shamans from the
Northwest Coast. In Native mythology, social outcasts would
often be rehabilitated by acquiring shamanistic powers.

through successive ordeals, and finally crowns his
career by marrying a proud woman who has killed
all her former suitors. Together they produce children who themselves become heroes.

The story of the orphan Sweet Medicine, told
by the Cheyenne of Wyoming and South Dakota,
also involves supernatural abilities. As a child,
Sweet Medicine provided a foretaste of his future
shamanistic powers (see pages 116–18) by causing
miraculous disappearances and indulging in
grossly antisocial behaviour. He capped this one
day when he performed a dance in which he cut
off his own head. His grandmother, who was his
guardian spirit, revived him on this occasion, but
such eccentric behaviour only served to alienate
him from society. His isolation grew deeper as he
approached adulthood. In a quarrel over a buffalo
skin, Sweet Medicine killed a powerful chief and

fled the village. Warriors attempted to hunt him
down, but he taunted his pursuers by appearing
and vanishing at will, successively transforming
himself into a coyote, a rabbit, a crow, an owl and
a blackbird.

When the Cheyenne finally succeeded in
confining Sweet Medicine to one location, his
response was to use his shamanistic powers to
retire for four years to the realm of the animal spirits. Here he persuaded the spirits to withhold the
animals that the Cheyenne hunted, so causing a
great famine among them. Eventually, he returned
and was moved to pity by some hungry children
that he encountered. After feeding them, he issued
instructions to the rest of the community about
how the destructive feud was to be healed. They
were to build a special lodge with a buffalo skull
in the centre. Once this had been accomplished,

The Boy and the Horse

A story told by the Pawnee people of the Plains region concerns a destitute boy whose compassion is ultimately rewarded with renown as a warrior. The rise of a person from humble origins to great prowess is a common theme of Native myths.

A poor boy lived with his grandmother on the outskirts of a village. The two were so impoverished that they were reduced to eating the soles of old moccasins and the remains of other people's food. On one occasion, near a campsite, the boy was dismayed to see people shooting at a nest of eagles.

Later, as the boy was scavenging, an eagle approached him. "Because you felt sorry for us, we will help you," it declared. First, the eagle led the boy to a tree, where he found some arrows. Then it directed him to a hill. An old, unkempt horse with swollen ankles was tethered there.

Despite the animal's woeful state, it had once belonged to a chief, and had been chosen by the eagles as a magical gift to the boy.

When the tribe was called upon to go to war, the mangy horse led the boy to a ravine. Here, it transformed itself into a vigorous young bay by rolling in the dust. It then commanded the boy to paint lightning symbols on its flanks as a sign of its supernatural origins, and they joined up with the war party. Riding the magic horse, the boy attacked and killed the enemy chief. He and the horse then promptly vanished.

When the boy reappeared, proclaiming his brave exploits, the incredulous villagers mocked him, as his horse had reverted to its decrepit state. Another battle ensued, with the same outcome. Finally, the boy went out for a third time to engage the enemy, and fought so fiercely that he put them to flight.

As the boy turned to leave the battlefield, his mount was joined first by a solitary grey steed and then by a great multitude of horses. The people recognized this as a sign of his glory, and hailed him as a great chief.

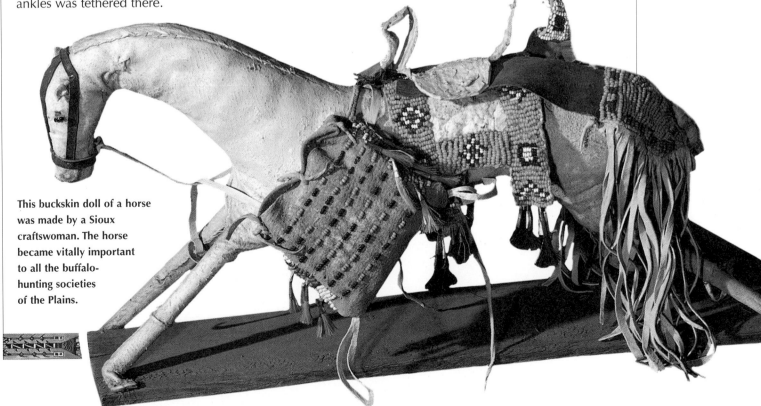

This buckskin doll of a horse was made by a Sioux craftswoman. The horse became vitally important to all the buffalo-hunting societies of the Plains.

A Hero's Attack on a Giant Elk

A characteristic role for many hero figures was as a guardian of the first humans on Earth. They attained this status by vanquishing threatening spirits and monsters. In a legend of the Jicarila Apache, the hero Jonayaiyin slays a monstrous beast that has been spreading terror among the people.

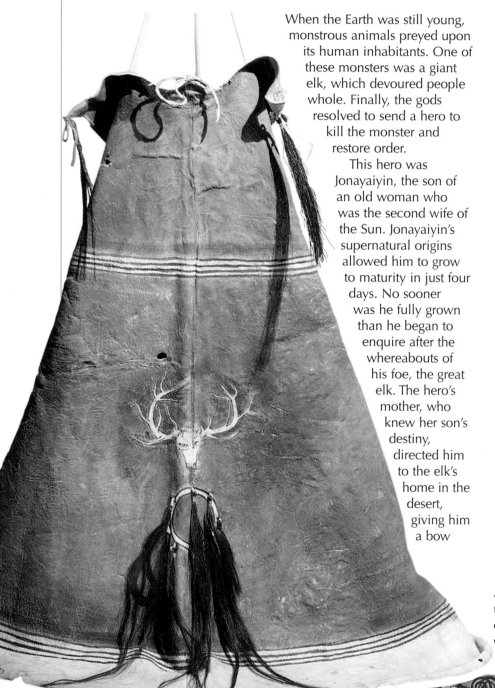

When the Earth was still young, monstrous animals preyed upon its human inhabitants. One of these monsters was a giant elk, which devoured people whole. Finally, the gods resolved to send a hero to kill the monster and restore order.

This hero was Jonayaiyin, the son of an old woman who was the second wife of the Sun. Jonayaiyin's supernatural origins allowed him to grow to maturity in just four days. No sooner was he fully grown than he began to enquire after the whereabouts of his foe, the great elk. The hero's mother, who knew her son's destiny, directed him to the elk's home in the desert, giving him a bow and arrows to accomplish his task. Jonayaiyin set out, reaching the elk's domain in four huge strides.

As Jonayaiyin lay in wait for the monster, the creatures of the desert came to ask him what he was doing there. When he told them, they offered him their help. Since the elk was lying in open grassland with no trees or bushes to cover Jonayaiyin's approach, the lizard gave him a lizard-skin disguise. The gopher then dug a tunnel, so that Jonayaiyin could attack the elk from below the ground. Jonayaiyin made his way through the tunnel and shot the elk straight through the heart. But the elk stuck its antlers into the tunnel and ploughed up vast amounts of earth, which are still visible to this day as mountains. As it pursued Jonayaiyin through the burrow, the desert spiders came to his aid. Wherever the elk chased him, the spiders put up webs to impede its progress. At last the elk collapsed with exhaustion, and the hero killed it. In doing so, he freed people from their fear and misery.

A Cheyenne model tipi decorated with the image of an elk. Before white encroachment, the American elk was widespread throughout the continent.

he appeared among them, and intoned sacred songs for four days and nights. At the end of this time, the hunters emerged from the lodge to find buffalo grazing in their village.

Having saved the Cheyenne from starvation, Sweet Medicine returned to the realm where the spirits of all living things on Earth coexist peacefully. During his sojourn with the spirits, he was granted long life and presented with a bundle containing four sacred arrows. He came back to the human world with them, and to this day they hang in the communal lodges of the Cheyenne, where they form the basis of their ritual observance and medicine ceremonies.

Sweet Medicine lived a number of lifetimes; his gift of longevity from the spirits meant that he could grow old and regain his youth several times. In a later addition to the ancient legend, he made various prophesies, predicting the extermination of the buffalo and the introduction of horses and cattle. In a tone that became progressively more tragic, he foretold the arrival of the white man, prophesying that the Cheyenne would not only fall subject to their control, but would eventually be supplanted by them. Sweet Medicine finally died during one of his recurring periods of rejuvenation. He was survived by his brother, who also lived for many generations.

Historical Heroes

Native American culture does not recognize any rigid distinction between myth and history: as well as such timeless heroes as Manabozho, several historical figures are regarded as legendary for their resistance to white encroachment. Real-life heroes shared with mythological ones the possession of magical or shamanic powers.

The earliest of the great warriors to offer concerted opposition to the colonists was Pontiac, an Ottawa chief who succeeded for a time in uniting no fewer than ten tribes in the Great Lakes region against the British. Pontiac was inspired by the revivalist cult of the Delaware shaman Neolin, who had travelled around the shores of Lake Erie in 1762, urging Indian communities to readopt their ancient beliefs. Pontiac's attack on Detroit in May 1763 caught the British completely by surprise, and led to a string of victories against colonial garrisons around the Great Lakes. The rebellion finally failed after two years, defeated not militarily but by a combination of plague and Indian disunity.

Further opposition was mounted in the first decade of the nineteenth century by two Shawnee brothers, Tenskwatawa (the "Shawnee Prophet") and Tecumseh. Establishing a settlement known as Prophet's Town in 1807, these leaders espoused a policy of returning to the old ways, but unlike Pontiac, did not aim to reconquer North America. Rather, they envisaged coexistence with the whites, arguing with the adminstration of the new United States (which had replaced British rule after the American Revolution of 1775–83) that the continent's original inhabitants had an incontrovertible right to their ancestral lands. Tenskwatawa became renowned as a visionary. In a series of trances, he claimed to have been shown a future paradise by the supreme deity, the Master of Life. On another occasion, he used a solar eclipse to convince onlookers of his ability to control natural forces. However, his power was broken when he led an ill-advised insurrection against the British, and was defeated. Tecumseh, on the other hand, continued the struggle against American federal forces with a combination of shrewd tactical judgement and persuasive oratory. His charismatic appeal was used to great advantage by the British, who formed an alliance with many of the northeastern tribes against the United States in the War of 1812. Tecumseh's forces scored notable successes before he was killed in battle. The mystique surrounding him was heightened by a premonition he received of his own death, and by the fact that his body was never recovered.

Several great Indian leaders of the later nineteenth century actively challenged forcible removals and relocations. One of the most extensive forced migrations was that of the Chiricahua Apache of the Southwest, which took place from the early 1870s onwards. For over twenty years, the Apache resisted displacement, led first by Victorio and then by the legendary Goyathlay (Geronimo; 1829–1909). Geronimo's rebellion of 1881–86 made extensive use of guerrilla tactics, prompting the US military to draft more than 5,000 men into the area. By the time he was finally forced to surrender in 1886, Geronimo's name had become synonymous with daring and effective military strategy. His persistent evasion of capture and the uncanny way in which he seemed to anticipate danger earned him a reputation for clairvoyance among his followers.

The Sioux of the Plains region were implacable opponents of the mass settlement of the West by whites that gained increasing momentum from the 1850s onwards. Many important leaders were to come to prominence during the course of the desperate struggle to resist the inexorable process of incursion, which lasted until the early 1890s. One of the principal strategists of this period was a young Oglala chief called Crazy Horse. Together with the Hunkpapa Sioux chief Sitting Bull, it was he who organized the Plains peoples' final stand, between 1876 and 1890, against the destruction of their culture (see pages 130–31). Both warriors were looked upon as "holy men" by their people, as a result of having experienced powerful visions that influenced their future actions.

The Hunkpapa Sioux chieftain Sitting Bull is shown in this photograph of 1885. For decades, he conducted a heroic defence of Sioux culture. Sitting Bull was killed by Native policemen while resisting arrest in 1890.

Crazy Horse's profound mistrust of whites came from his witnessing, at an early age, a savage reprisal raid on a settlement of the Brulé Sioux. Following this incident, Crazy Horse went into the wilderness to undertake a vision quest (see pages 116–19). A trance that he induced through self-castigation brought him a vision of a warrior who had a lightning streak painted on his face and wore a hawk's skin in his hair. On reaching maturity and distinguishing himself as a fearless warrior, Crazy Horse always joined battle dressed in this way. His name was said to have its origin in a later vision (see page 119).

The famous Sioux chief Sitting Bull won a reputation for honour and selflessness at an early age, killing his first buffalo calf and distributing the meat to needy people when only ten years old. As a man, during his long campaign against the whites, he carried with him a sacred buffalo skull, and invoked the animal's protective spirit. While on a vision quest at Medicine Deer Rock in Montana, he foresaw his great victory at the Battle of Little Bighorn in 1876.

Though the heroic stature of these historical figures is unquestioned, it did not rest primarily on any perceived superhuman powers. Rather, to their followers they epitomized the human qualities of honour and resourcefulness held dear by Native American cultures.

Demons and Monsters

In Native American mythology, gigantic or grotesque creatures usually occupy the familiar role of terrifying, destructive beings feared by both people and animals. Less commonly, however, they are also thought to exercise a beneficent, creative influence.

The legend of the Earth as Turtle Island that is found in many Native traditions shows a gigantic creature in a benevolent light. For example, a myth of the Lenape of the Northeast narrates how the world required a support once it had been made, and how a giant turtle was designated to fill this role. Thereafter, the Earth has rested stably on the back of this mighty reptile.

More surprisingly, however, monsters that are normally associated with destruction also played an integral part in the creation of the world. In the myths of a number of peoples, vital aspects of the world as we know it emanated from a primal monster. Thus, tribes of the Great Plateau (the area immediately inland from the Northwest Coast) believe that all Native American peoples sprang from the body of a single huge creature, whose form was unspecified.

Similarly, a creation legend of the Nez Percé tells of the existence, at the beginning of time, of a monster whose body covered much of the Great Plateau. Whenever the creature inhaled, it sucked in everything that stood in its path – grass, trees, animals, even the wind. When the Trickster Coyote learned that all the creatures of the earth had vanished, he travelled to where the monster lay, taking with him knives, and tools for kindling fire, which he intended to use as weapons against the beast. As he approached the monster, Coyote allowed himself to be sucked inside too. There, he found most of the animals still alive, but driven wild by their predicament.

Coyote eventually succeeded in calming the enraged and frightened animals and solicited their help. First, he ordered some children to lead him to the monster's heart, where he began to slice off fat to feed the starving creatures and to fuel a fire, which he laid under the heart and proceeded to light. As the heat increased, the monster begged Coyote to desist, promising to release him in return, but Coyote was intent on killing the beast and freeing all the trapped animals. He hacked away at the heart, breaking the blades of all his knives, but finally managed to tear it out. In its death throes, the monster opened all its orifices and the animals escaped. They took with them the bones of those who had perished inside the creature's body, which Coyote had insisted they gather up before they left.

Once outside the monster, Coyote sprinkled blood on the bones, and all the dead animals came to life again in an instant. Next he dismembered the monster's body, flinging portions of it to all the points of the compass. From these sprang all the various tribes of the Plateau, each residing in their separate domains. However, no sooner had Coyote used up all the flesh than he realized that he had forgotten to account for the area where he was standing. So, taking some water, he rinsed his hands, and from this mixture of blood and water, the Nez Percé were created.

Used in curing rituals by the Iroquois False Face Society (see page 120), these turtle-shell shaman's rattles recall the monstrous animal that was believed to carry the Earth on its back.

89

Buffalo hides can be seen laid out to dry in this image of daily life on the Plains by a Hidatsa artist. Myths relate how the first people had to learn to subdue the buffalo, which was once a predatory animal.

Other dangerous creatures of the primordial world were rendered harmless by the brave intervention of humans. For example, the Arikara Pawnee of the Plains tell a story of a man-eating buffalo that terrorized the first inhabitants of the Earth until it was overcome. These first people, who came out of the Earth, hunted and ate many different kinds of animal, but had not yet encountered the buffalo. Eventually, on their travels, they came across a lake, from which emerged a buffalo-like horned monster which they called Cut-Nose. Both Cut-Nose and the buffaloes that sprang from its body were ferocious, pursuing the people and killing many of them. For a while, the people held them in check by creating deep canyons, but the buffaloes always managed to circumvent these obstacles and slaughter their victims at will.

The slaughter was finally halted when people learned to defend themselves. A young man, alarmed by overhearing the beasts planning a massacre, fled to the hills. Here, he encountered a stranger who instructed him in the use of the bow and arrow and told him to pass this knowledge on to his people. The next time that the marauding buffaloes emerged from the Earth, the people conducted a furious assault on them with the weapons they had made. They succeeded in killing many of the animals and put the rest to flight. Ever since that time, buffaloes have been the hunted rather than the hunters.

Sacred and Terrifying Creatures

Many Native American cultures have myths of primeval monsters that conduct a reign of terror before being overcome. Yet the horrifying, grotesque nature of certain monsters does not preclude them from being venerated as spiritual beings.

In North America, there are dangerous and unpleasant creatures aplenty, such as poisonous reptiles, spiders or mosquitoes. However, Native myths rarely bemoan their existence, but rather assign them a role in the drama of humans, animals and spirit beings.

The terrifying monsters of Native American mythology are of two basic types. First, there are giant, or otherwise only slightly altered, versions of familiar species. Secondly, there are fantastic beings that bear only a remote resemblance to humans or animals. Tales concerning the first type of monster are generally straightforward. Many archaic stories introduce primeval versions of well-known animals that are more threatening than their modern counterparts – telling, for example, of carnivorous ravens, deer and caribou, or of predators with enhanced powers. Thus one Alaskan Inuit myth describes a ten-legged polar bear. Such stories customarily follow an established pattern: the animal's career of predation is followed either by its destruction or by its transformation into a familiar form.

A common myth is that of the giant bird; on the Northwest Coast and in Alaska, numerous legends tell of eagles so huge that they carry off whales to feed their young. Similarly, a Southeastern myth concerns a giant turkey that once preyed on humans. At a meeting called to discuss how to destroy the bird, the people chose a black snake and a puppy to lead the attack. When the turkey next alighted, the snake rushed forward and tried to whip it, but missed. The puppy then ran at the monster from behind and knocked it over, whereupon the men closed in and clubbed it to death. From then on, turkeys were easy to hunt and kill.

Fantastic creatures are particularly prevalent in Alaskan Inuit mythology. This tradition venerates several kinds of monstrous or grotesque figures as spirit beings. Some Inuit myths are about subterranean or submarine spirit "people" who either help humans by providing them with animals to hunt, or punish those who transgress against sacred laws by ensuring that game animals suddenly become scarce. One such group of spirits was under the control of a hybrid being,

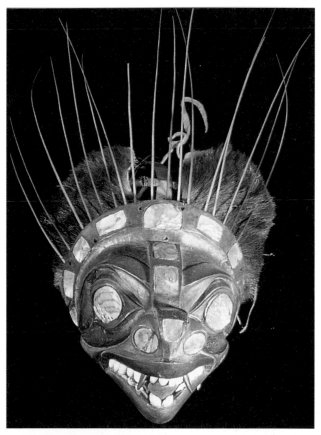

A Tlingit headdress representing the sea monster Gonaquadet, a transforming spirit that brings fortune to some fishermen and hunters, and death to others.

half-man and half-wolf, whose constant companion was a grotesque, dwarfish creature with immense ears designed to listen to human activity above ground. Success in hunting involved enlisting the co-operation of these spirits. Similarly, whale hunting among the Inuit was associated with a myth in which a Trickster raven harpooned a nameless whale-like sea beast; after it had expired, the beast's body changed into the land inhabited by the whale hunters. As a result of this transformation, the Inuit regarded both the beast and their homeland as sacred.

The fearsome Thunderbird is depicted here in a Kwakiutl ceremonial costume. The dancer wearing this imposing garb would appear with a loud screeching and flapping of wings.

Another sacred monster was the great horned snake of the Mississippi valley. Excavations of many burial sites and temple mounds along the river (see page 48) have uncovered evidence of a cult devoted to a horned or plumed serpent. A story narrated by the Cheyenne gives one account of the origin of this fearsome yet sacred being. Two young men who were journeying together came across two immense eggs lying on the prairie. One of them refused to touch the eggs, but the other, overcome with hunger, built a fire and cooked them. The men set off again, but the one who had eaten began to feel sick. Presently his legs grew heavy and he noticed that the skin on them had become dark and scaly. They continued their journey, but the man was becoming more like a snake and was gradually reduced to crawling, and then dragging his body. He felt a powerful urge to swim and, when they stopped by a lake, he spent all night splashing and writhing in the water. By this time, only his head and arms were still those of a human. He heard the spirits calling him to the Mississippi River, and asked his friend to help him get there.

After enduring many hardships, the two companions finally reached the great river as night was falling. Exhausted, the friend of the snake-man immediately fell asleep. When he awoke in the morning, he heard a voice calling to him from the river. Glancing towards the water, he saw that his friend had been transformed into a great snake with blue skin and two horns protruding from its head. "This is where I belong, my friend," said the snake-man. "My body will lie along the river bed for all eternity." Saying this, the serpent told his friend to instruct the people in how he should be venerated: "Everyone who comes to the river should bring with them fine meat and good tobacco, and drop these offerings in midstream. If they observe this courtesy, I will give them my blessing." Thereafter, whenever Cheyenne people crossed the Mississippi they followed these rules, and so gained the benefit of the river serpent's favour.

The Child-eating Ogress of Oregon

A story about a monster that devours children is told by the Wasco people from the Columbia River region in Oregon. Like many such tales, it combines serious and comic elements. While evoking childhood terrors of the unseen and the unknown, at the same time it presents the object of fear as stupid and clumsy. The story's central character is the Atatalia, a hideous ogress whose gargantuan body is covered in spots and stripes.

A brother and sister were out gathering flints, when the little girl became scared: "Hurry," she said, "or the Atatalia might get us!" But no sooner had she spoken than she looked around, and saw the Atatalia. The children ran as fast as their legs could carry them, but the ogress caught them and put them in her great basket, which she tied securely shut. She then set off home to feed her own children on these two tasty morsels.

In the basket, the boy's foot began to itch painfully from where the girl was sitting on it. "Sister," he said, "you're hurting my foot where I have an itch." The Atatalia misheard this for something that sounded very similar in the Wasco language, and asked, alarmed, "What is the matter? Are my children burning up?" Immediately, the girl saw a way to frighten the monster and gain their release, so she responded: "Your children are burning up, for sure!" Terrified, the monster woman hung up her basket on the branch of an oak tree and started to run home. As

soon as she had gone, the children took a flint, cut the strings of the basket cover and clambered out. Filling the basket with stones and dirt, they hung it up again and ran to the river.

When the Atatalia came back from her fruitless journey, she took down the basket without checking, put it on her back and returned home once more, where she discovered that the children had escaped. She immediately set out again to recapture them.

The boy, who had magical powers, placed five rivers as obstacles in the monster's path. The Atatalia jumped the first river with ease, but enjoyed it so much that she repeated her leap five times, and did the same at the next four. Finally, she spied the children ahead of her, and breathed in to drag them backwards. But as soon as she breathed out again, the children flew off ahead of her.

When they came to the Columbia river, the children jumped into a canoe. They implored the fish to eat the

Atatalia and the cliffs to crush her. When the monster reached the river, she waded in and tried in vain to suck the canoe towards her. Then the fish began to nibble her body, and the rocks came crashing down on her. At length, the stupid ogress gave up and waded off to nurse her wounds, leaving the children to make good their escape.

Humans and Animals

The relationship between humans and animals was fundamental to all aspects of Native American life. For most peoples, survival without animals would have been impossible. Meat, skin, bone, sinew, feather and ivory supplied almost all the essential needs of daily existence.

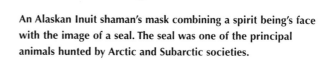

An Alaskan Inuit shaman's mask combining a spirit being's face with the image of a seal. The seal was one of the principal animals hunted by Arctic and Subarctic societies.

Aside from their practical utility, animals also played a vital role in the spiritual life of Native American communities. Animals, after all, had been present at the creation and were thought to embody certain aspects of that mythical time. In some regards, animals were even envied: whereas humans, in order to feed and clothe themselves, had arduously to hunt and gather, animals fed at relative leisure and did not need to make clothing and weapons.

Importantly, all animals were believed to possess souls. Some – notably, such big-game animals as the buffalo, eagle and bear – had powerful spirits that could help people or harm them according to how they were treated. Animals were therefore revered as holy beings. However, there was no contradiction in the universal Indian view that the sacred and beautiful must also be hunted, killed and eaten.

It was essential for human beings to gain an intimate knowledge of the animal kingdom. Every Native American growing up in a traditional society acquired, from an early age, an immense store of wisdom about the natural history of the fauna in their locality. This included an understanding of animal behaviour, anatomy, feeding patterns, breeding habits and migratory cycles. Combined with this knowledge was a repertory of specialized hunting techniques; to learn these required intense intellectual and physical application. To hunt successfully meant adapting knowledge to specific situations, together with a detailed understanding of topography and environment. The consummate hunter knew where and when to stalk his prey, and at what precise moment to strike in any given weather conditions. Moreover, this body of practical knowledge was underpinned by a rich fund of myth, legend, songs, rituals and local history. Without it, a hunter could not place his actions in context. To hunt, therefore, meant infinitely more than simply killing and eating. Rather, it was an act fraught with complex rules of conduct and spiritual significance.

To Native Americans, therefore, hunting combined a high degree of flexibility and initiative with a strict observation of social and religious conventions. In some cultures, the male hunter is symbolized by the moon, because, in contrast to the sun, which follows a fixed course, the moon wanders through the sky, "like a man, a hunter: going where he wants, seldom in the same place for long".

Summoning the Buffalo to Aid the Hunter

For a major undertaking such as a buffalo hunt, the Plains people undertook spiritual preparations that were as meticulously detailed as the tactics of the chase itself. Apache hunters were typical in their care over the correct hunting and butchering techniques.

The Apache would begin their preparations for hunting by praying that the guardian spirit of the buffalo would ensure a plentiful supply of animals. The hunters lit a sacred pipe and petitioned the animal's spirit with the following wish: "There will be many. There will be much meat. We will camp among them."

The people would then sing and dance in honour of the buffalo, mimicking the animal's horns by putting their hands to their heads.

At times when the herds were scarce, the Apache observed a special hunting ritual, conducted by the community's shaman. A piece of level ground was prepared, on which the shaman would scatter dung and pollen. As the people prayed, he performed four songs and imitated the bellowing of buffalo.

At the conclusion of a successful hunt, butchering had to be conducted according to a stringent procedure, lest the animal's soul be offended and its companions avoid future hunters. First, the hide was cut along the right shoulder. The foreleg and shoulder were then severed. A slice of fatty meat was cut from the back and thrown towards the east as an offering to the animal's spirit. The remainder of the animal was turned into food and clothing.

Care and reverence were shown even in dealing with the rest of the carcass. The feet, in particular, were treated with great respect, for fear of incurring the wrath of the spirit and being trampled by the herd's hooves on the next hunt.

A painting of a Buffalo Dance among Plains peoples by the artist George Catlin (1794–1872).

Animal Spouses and Guardians

Almost all Native North American societies have myths concerning human and animal marriages. The human spouse may be male or female, and the animal partner is usually one of the larger mammals or birds. The range of species into which legendary people marry is extensive, including buffalo, deer, brown bear, dog, whale, eagle and gull.

There is an abundance of Inuit stories that tell of wandering heroes who are married to a succession of animals. In one such tale, the hero weds a polar bear, a brown bear and a whale. After a brief liaison, each animal wife is destroyed, while the husband himself narrowly escapes death. Thus, although these relationships initiate the hero into the spirit world of animals, their violent end shows how they violated the natural order.

The same ambiguity is present in an Inuit story of the swan maidens. This recounts how a man once approached a lake where some swans, who had shed their clothes and adopted the guise of women, were bathing. Concealing the feathered garments of one of the swan-women, the man took her to his home, where they lived happily together and raised children. One day, however,

the woman discovered her swan-skin and fled, taking her children with her. When the man tracked them down, his wife feigned death to escape his wrath. But during the ensuing burial, she rose up from the grave, and he struck her dead. He also killed several of the swans who were in attendance.

However, when relationships between humans and animals were completely harmonious, even death could be overcome and the animals' souls reborn. A myth of the Thompson Indians of British Columbia tells of one such happy human–animal marriage. A renowned deer hunter harboured a deep love of the animals that he hunted. One day, as he was following some tracks through the forest, he came upon a woman who confessed her love for him and led him to her underground lair in the hills. There, the hunter was welcomed as the woman's husband by deer in human guise. The following day, they asked him to go hunting; he agreed, and returned with two young deer for them. The deer people were overjoyed and ate the meat he had provided. At the end of the meal, they said to the hunter, "We have saved every bone. Now take them to the water." He did

A stone carving by the 19th-century Haida sculptor Skaowskeag depicting the Bear Mother myth. This tale relates how the daughter of a chief was punished for cursing bears. The half-human, half-bear children that she had by her bear spouse had sharp claws and teeth, which made breastfeeding excruciatingly painful.

96

as he was instructed, and the two deer immediately sprang to life again.

At length, when the deer woman had given birth to a son, she and her husband agreed that the time had come for them to visit his people. So, she magically condensed some provisions into a small bundle, and they set off. Once they had arrived in the village where the husband's people lived, they treated the villagers to a sumptuous feast. Although the hunter and the deer woman stayed for a time among the people, they finally returned to the deer; the man eventually became one of them. However, his son remained in the village, teaching the people how to hunt and to observe the proper rituals that ensured that their prey would always be reborn.

The Elk Guardian Spirit

Native American hunters were guided by a rigid code of ethics. Lying or boasting about hunting prowess was forbidden, as was killing more animals than the individual or community required. Anyone transgressing these rules would be punished by the guardian spirit of the animals. A story of the Wasco of the Northwest Coast stresses the importance of observing this code.

A boy who hunted squirrels and birds was once upbraided by his boastful father: "When I was your age, I hunted elks." Pointing to a scar on his forehead, he lied, "An elk did this." In fact, he had gashed it stumbling into a tree.

The young man soon became a proficient hunter. He had gained the protection of a she-elk, who told him: "If you serve me, I will be your guardian spirit. But you must not kill too many animals."

Nevertheless, his father continued to mock his son's meagre tally of kills. At this, the elk lost patience and had her protégé slaughter five elk herds. But his bloodlust was so great that he turned on his guardian. She ran into a lake and, feigning death, sank below the water as he clung to her.

An elk painted on the side of a Zuni water jar. This animal – also known as the wapiti – was once widely hunted in North America.

At the bottom of the lake, the man came to his senses, and saw countless elk in the guise of people. A voice called, "Draw him in." The hunter was drawn to the side of his guardian, who said: "Why did you exceed my command? Do you see all the elk-people that you have killed? Your father lied. Tree bark cut him, not an elk's horn. I can no longer be your guardian." Then another voice cried: "Cast him out!" and the young man was sent back to his village. He lay in bed five days and nights and then called for water. "Heat water and wash me. Call my friends so that I may talk to them. And bring five elk-skins."

When the people had assembled, the hunter told them: "My father was dissatisfied because I did not do as he had done. His wishes grieved the guardian spirit that helped me. My father said that he had been scarred by an elk. He wanted me to kill more than was needed. The spirit has left me." With that, he died.

97

The Vulnerability of Animals

While Native American myths attribute power and dignity to animals, especially the larger species, there is also an awareness in some narratives of their comparative weakness and their dependence upon human help.

One of the quintessential Native American symbols of power was the eagle. Its sheer size and majesty, and the proximity to the heavens of both its flight and its nesting places, gave rise to many myths. Yet a Navajo story about an eagle hunt combines a recognition of the bird's power with a reminder of its vulnerability.

Two young men hunting deer stopped to watch an eagle. They observed as the bird soared away into the hills. The next day a party of hunters discovered its eyrie at a site known as Standing Rock. The men saw two eagle chicks in a nest on a precipice and decided to capture them, but the only way to reach the nest would be to let a person in a basket down onto the ledge, a perilous undertaking that none of the hunters dared risk.

Living in the village was a scrawny youth called He-Who-Picks-Up, who was chosen for the task. He was given a fine meal of bread, corn and meat, and told: "You will eat like this for the rest of your life, if you agree to get the eagles." The boy agreed, and was lowered down to the nest. Just then, the wind spoke to him. "These people are lying. Once they have the eagles, they will abandon you. Get into the nest and stay." So, when he was close enough, He-Who-Picks-Up

An eagle is one of the figures carved on this totem pole in the village of Kispiox in British Columbia.

climbed into the nest. The other people tried in vain to get him to throw down the eagle chicks to them. Next day they returned and attempted to coax him out of the nest, all to no avail. On the third day, threats and burning arrows failed to dislodge him. On the fourth day they left him to die. Half dead with terror, exhaustion and thirst, He-Who-Picks-Up sat till nightfall, when he heard the adult eagles returning to their eyrie. "Thanks, my child," they greeted him. "You have not thrown down your younger brothers!" And they dubbed the boy Chief-of-Eagles-in-the-Sky.

In gratitude, the father eagle fed the boy with corn meal and then, producing from his tail feathers a plant rich in water, quenched his raging thirst. Presently, the boy fell asleep between the parent birds, who had taken off their feathered robes to reveal that they had the bodies of humans. In the morning, other eagles assembled, and resolved to give the boy the same power that they had. They placed forked lightning under his feet, a sunbeam beneath his knees, strips of straight lightning under his chest and his outstretched arms, and a rainbow under his forehead. An eagle took hold of each end of the lightning strips and they soared away from the eyrie.

The Man Who Lived with Bears

A story told by the Skidi Pawnee people of the Plains shows that an intense feeling of kinship could exist between humans and other species. Such relationships were thought to be reciprocal: in this tale, the kindness shown by a person to a vulnerable bear is later rewarded.

A man out hunting once came upon an abandoned bear cub. Instead of killing the cub, he tied an offering of tobacco round its neck and blessed it, saying: "May Tirawa (the Supreme Deity) protect you!" After returning to his camp, he described to his pregnant wife what had happened, and when she later gave birth, their son grew up feeling a powerful sense of kinship with bears. So strongly did he identify with them that often, while alone, he would pray to bears' souls.

When the boy reached manhood, he was killed and dismembered in an enemy ambush. A male and a female bear found his remains and revived him with the help of supernatural powers. The man was completely restored and lived for a long while with his benefactors. During this time, he came to revere bears as the greatest and wisest of all beings, with the most powerful souls. The bears, however, reminded him of their place in the order of things. Their wisdom, they said, was a gift from Tirawa.

Eventually, the time came for the man to return to his people. As he took his leave, the male bear embraced him, pressed its mouth to the man's lips, and

rubbed him with its paws and fur. The touch of the fur gave the man power, while the kiss gave him wisdom. He became a great warrior and established the Bear Dance among his people.

A Plains medicine man of the Blackfoot tribe is shown wearing a bearskin in this 1832 painting by George Catlin. Shamans from many peoples invoked the power of the bear's spirit in healing the sick.

ON THE WARPATH

In warfare between tribes warriors were granted their strength in battle from the spirit world that is described in myth. Power came to warriors in visions, and battle plans were often laid according to how a chief's dreams were interpreted. Ceremonies to ensure success were sometimes performed by shamans. Even the garments of war, decorated with symbols and patterns, were thought to offer protection, and headdresses were made from the feathers of sacred birds of prey. Each bird had different attributes – swiftness, vigilance, keen eyesight. When the white man's conquest of the continent was almost complete, Native American devotees of the Ghost Dance tried to ward off bullets with sacred shirts.

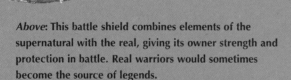

Above: **This battle shield combines elements of the supernatural with the real, giving its owner strength and protection in battle. Real warriors would sometimes become the source of legends.**

FAC SIMILE EINER INDIANISCHEN MALEREI.   FAC SIMILE D'UNE PEINTURE INDIENNE.
FAC SIMILE OF AN INDIAN PAINTING

Left: **Warriors were highly esteemed for their spiritual powers and brought honour to their people, although tribal battles were not often recorded in myth. This depiction of a bloody combat is reproduced in Karl Bodmer's *Travels into the Interior of North America*, 1832–34.**

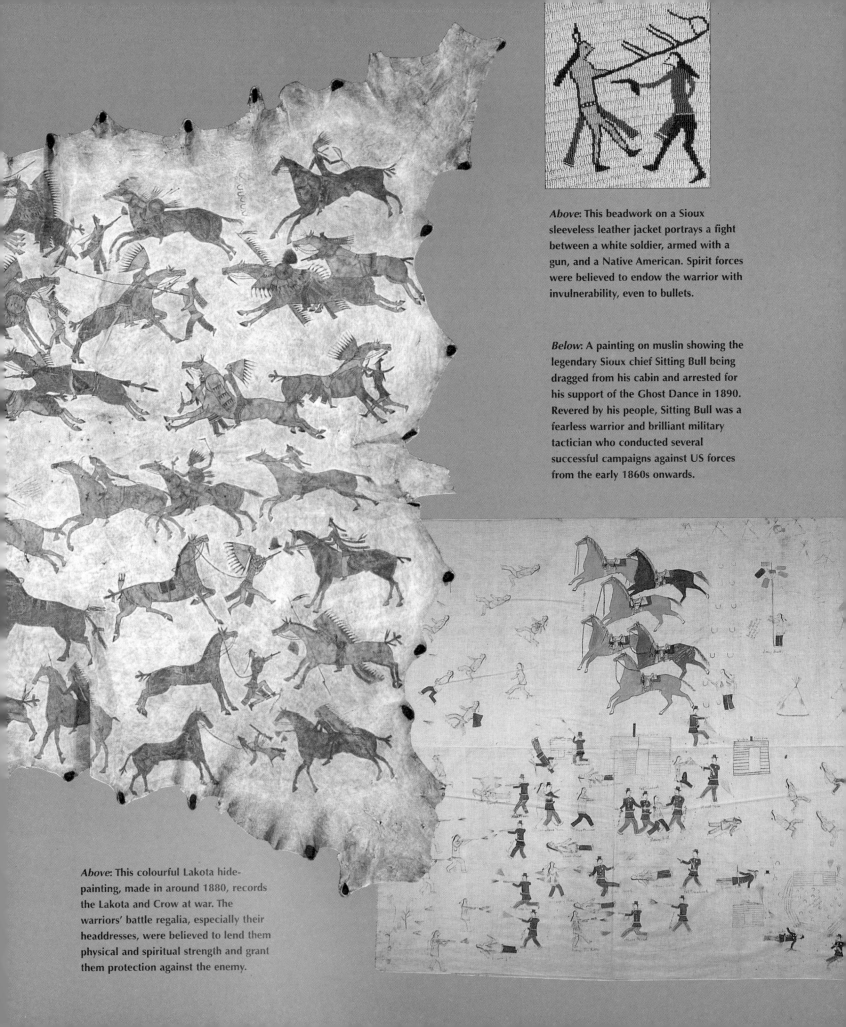

Above: This beadwork on a Sioux sleeveless leather jacket portrays a fight between a white soldier, armed with a gun, and a Native American. Spirit forces were believed to endow the warrior with invulnerability, even to bullets.

Below: A painting on muslin showing the legendary Sioux chief Sitting Bull being dragged from his cabin and arrested for his support of the Ghost Dance in 1890. Revered by his people, Sitting Bull was a fearless warrior and brilliant military tactician who conducted several successful campaigns against US forces from the early 1860s onwards.

Above: This colourful Lakota hide-painting, made in around 1880, records the Lakota and Crow at war. The warriors' battle regalia, especially their headdresses, were believed to lend them physical and spiritual strength and grant them protection against the enemy.

Totems and Clans

Native American societies on the fertile and prosperous Pacific Northwest Coast were structured according to a system of clans – groups of related families – arranged within an elaborate hierarchy. Each clan traced its origin to an animal spirit, or totem. Prominent clans would proclaim their status and sacred lineage by erecting huge carved poles outside their communal houses, decorated with the animal crests of the families who dwelt within.

Northwest Coast peoples such as the Kwakiutl, Tsimshian, Haida and Tlingit, who inhabit an area now covered by Washington State, British Columbia and southeast Alaska, have always been favoured by an abundance of edible flora and fauna. Because it is sheltered by mountain ranges from the Subarctic interior to the east, and because the sea is warmed by the Japan Current, this narrow coastal region enjoys a rainy, temperate climate that makes it very fertile.

There was an enormous variety of sea and freshwater fish, marine mammals and land animals available to the hunter-gatherer societies that flourished along this coast, reflected in the region's mythology and art. Moreover, the extensive forest habitats of the bear, deer, elk and moose yielded abundant timber for housing, tools and artefacts; red and durable yellow cedarwood were the favoured materials.

The most striking examples of Northwest Coast art are the totem poles that served both as signs of clan affiliation and as ancestral monuments. These towering sculptures were visible from both sea and land and embodied the spiritual heritage of their owners in a number of different ways. The largest structures were freestanding memorial poles which were erected in honour of a dead chief; these began to be carved only in the nineteenth century, as Northwest Coast tribes acquired machine-made metal tools from their

An elaborately carved and painted totem pole in Vancouver, British Columbia. The principal figure at the top of this pole is Thunderbird, the fearsome spirit that brings rain, thunder and lightning.

How Raven Helped to Make Clans

Myths of the Tlingit trace the origin of their clan crests back to the beginning of time. At that period, the great deity Raven-at-the-head-of-Nass lived in darkness at the mouth of the Nass river, hoarding the sun, moon and stars in wooden boxes.

The sister of Raven-at-the-head-of-Nass gave birth to a son. This was the Trickster Raven (see pages 78–79), one of whose exploits was to steal the box of daylight from the deity.

After taking the box, the Raven Trickster offered it to people in exchange for food. But, meeting with only scorn and derision because they did not believe that it contained light, he opened the lid. With a roar, the sun burst out and rose into the sky, and the terrified people scattered in all directions.

The advent of daylight transformed creatures into the physical forms they have today. People who were clad in the skins of otters, beavers and seals turned into those animals. Those who were wearing nothing when the light arrived remained as human beings, and selected their clan crests in memory of their transformed companions.

The myth of Raven's theft of the sun is shown in this Taku Tlingit headdress. Daylight is represented by the inlaid mirror, and the disc of the Sun rests between Raven's ears.

trade with whites. However, these were only the last flowering of a carving tradition that reached back some 1,200 years. The first examples of such work were found on the interior posts and frontal poles of large communal dwellings.

Similar poles were made for the ashes of dead chiefs or other noblemen. The tops of these poles had a recess or casket which contained their cremated remains. The erection of a memorial or mortuary pole was an important ceremonial occasion.

The intricate designs on totem poles were far more than simple ornament. They derived from two interrelated sources, in human society and in the realm of myth. Northwest Coast societies were organized hierarchically into clans, each with its own chief and its separate domestic and ceremonial centre. Every clan traced its lineage back to an encounter in mythical time with a particular animal spirit, who had endowed the group with his power and bestowed on it his image for use as a

A community house (left) and Thunderbird totem pole from the Southern Kwakiutl settlement of Alert Bay, on Vancouver Island. Featuring on both exterior poles and on numerous carved posts within the communal dwellings, animal motifs stressed the clan's affiliation.

heraldic device. Thus, in southeast Alaska, Tlingit society was composed of two major moieties, or divisions: the Raven and the Eagle (though, among the southern Tlingit, the Eagle was replaced by the Wolf moiety). Within each moiety were further family subdivisions, with their own animal crests. Apart from the raven itself, crests of the Raven moiety showed the hawk, moose, sealion, whale, salmon and frog. And, in addition to the principal animal, Eagle and Wolf moiety crests included images of the brown bear, killer whale, dogfish and halibut. All artefacts, however great or small, from house posts and totem poles to bowls, spoons, ladles and woven ceremonial blankets, were densely covered with a multitude of animal designs associated with the owner's clan.

Given their vital role in conveying information from generation to generation about a clan's supernatural provenance, crest designs were jealously guarded by those who owned them. If they were lost, whether captured as war trophies or surrendered as compensation for the murder of another clan member, clans spared no effort or expense to redeem them.

Northwest Coast Ceremonies

Among Northwest Coast peoples there were secret societies of shamans, whose ceremonies invoked the powers of patron spirits. The social functions of the clan and the society were quite different: whereas clans emphasized the hierarchical divisions between people, societies cut across these groupings, and their rituals stressed common ancestry.

In most Northwest Coast cultures, elaborate winter ceremonies were conducted, both in order to express and reinforce lineage traditions and to display clan crests. For example, each year the Hamatsa (or Cannibal) Society of the Kwakiutl (see page 122) re-enacted in a ceremony the ancient encounter between their ancestors and Baxbaxwalanuxsiwe, the "Cannibal-at-the-North-End-of-the-World". Initiates derived power from their patron spirit in a series of dramatic, frenzied dances.

Many of these events included potlatch ceremonies marking a rite of passage, at which tribal chiefs, as a sign of their material wealth, would donate (or even burn) food, skins, blankets and other possessions.

The Haida village of Ninstints in the southern Queen Charlotte Islands. As well as crest poles and tall memorial poles, mortuary poles surmounted by chests containing ancestral remains can be seen. Shortly after this photograph was taken, in the late 19th century, the village was devastated by diseases.

Dances and dance pantomimes played an especially important role in ceremonial events. Every detail of the choreography and the accompanying songs told genealogical stories. The dances of the Kwakiutl, perhaps the most intricate and spectacular of these ceremonies, gave rise to one of the richest forms of Northwest Coast art — the dance mask (see pages 82–83). Usually covering the whole face or just the forehead, these wooden masks sometimes incorporated moveable parts or faces within faces that were revealed at critical moments. While woodcarvers from other cultures in the region tended to decorate their work in one or two restrained colours, Kwakiutl artists employed a rich palette of dazzling combinations. These pigments, together with the use of inlaid stone and shell and undulating fibrous materials, produced dramatic effects in the firelight that

A Tlingit wooden frog clan hat of about 1820, decorated with inlays of abalone shell. Each woven ring represents a potlatch, or gift-giving feast, that the owner of the hat has sponsored.

illuminated the vast, crowded communal houses in which the ceremonies took place.

In the guise of their lineage animals, performers would take to the floor, mimicking the call and movements of their particular ancestral creatures. The dancers wore masks representing different birds, animals and imaginary beings. Of all the many masks, those depicting the legendary beasts were the most striking: among them were the fearsome sea-monster Sisiutl, the Thunderbird, and Hokhokw, a supernatural bird with a massive beak that could split men's skulls.

In addition to dancing, important rituals and initiations were undertaken during the winter ceremonies. For example, among the northern Kwakiutl, a supernatural wolf required that masked members of its lineage should enact wolf-spirit possession. This entailed wild and alarming behaviour in and around the village. Similarly, the Nootka of Vancouver Island enacted a wolf ritual that recalled the initiation, by a wolf, of their lineage ancestor. Dances, songs, masks and special whistles used during the ceremony were all based around this ancestor's visionary experience. Like the Kwakiutl ceremony, the Nootka rite was long, vivid and complex. It began with the blowing of special whistles outside the village, at which point wolf society novices, usually children, were carried off to a secret place where they were taught dances, songs and other clan lore. When they reappeared, led by masked wolf clan initiates, they were dressed in new ceremonial costumes and family crest masks and were called upon to demonstrate what they had learned during their initiation.

Intriguingly, the Nootka were virtually the only Northwest Coast people to hunt whales. In common with other whaling societies, the Nootka observed elaborate rituals that were intended both to lure the whales and to propitiate the souls of those harpooned and killed. Together with other peoples of the region, they believed that the spirits of the wolf and the whale were closely related. The grounds for this belief have become obscured by time, but it was widely held that reverence to the wolf would also please the whale. Therefore, the wolf rituals of the Nootka made explicit reference to the whales that would be hunted, under conditions of strict taboo and long ceremonial preparation, later in the year. Whale lineage crests were never used by these people, however.

The spirit-helpers who aided both shamans and laiety and who permitted their likenesses to be used as clan crests (see pages 103–4) were almost invariably non-prey animals or creatures that were only marginal to subsistence. Important crest animals included the raven, killer whale, grizzly bear, octopus and frog. For a variety of reasons both practical and spiritual, hunters would avoid killing these animals. For example, not only was the raven inedible, it was also too highly regarded in its role as a creator-hero (see page 78). The killer whale was regarded with reverential fear, while the grizzly bear was not hunted on account of its having a highly dangerous and unpredictable character.

A Tlingit myth describes the spirit origin of the frog crest. In the middle of a lake near Yakutat was a marshy reed bed where frogs used to sit. One day the daughter of the chief of the town made offensive remarks to the frogs about their sexual behaviour. That night a young man appeared to her and asked if she would marry him. The young woman had hitherto rejected every other suitor, but was instantly captivated by

A Tlingit shaman from the village of Chilkat, photographed in the late 19th century. He is holding a rattle carved in the form of a raven, one of the principal crest animals and spirit-helpers.

this handsome man – who was in fact a frog in human form. Pointing to the lake, the frog-man said: "My father's house lies just over there." "How fine it looks," replied the woman. As she and her new spouse approached the lake, it appeared to her as though a door in the house were opening to let them in; in reality, however, they were sinking below the waters of the lake.

When the woman's family and friends realized that she had disappeared, they began to bemoan her loss. The following spring, a hunter spotted her sitting among the frogs in the middle of the lake. The family gave many offerings in an attempt to persuade the frogs to release their kinswoman, but their efforts were all in vain. The people then tried a different approach, and started to dig trenches in order to drain the lake. As the water gushed out, it swept the frogs away, carrying the frog-bride with them. Taking care not to harm any of the frogs, the woman's family pulled her out of the water and attempted to restore her to her former self. However, she never recovered from her experience in the realm of the animals, and died shortly afterwards.

Following this sad affair, people and frogs grew closer to one another. They came to understand each other's languages, and the woman's family made great efforts to learn the frogs' songs and names. Future generations of the clan adopted a frog crest as a sign of this ancient supernatural connection.

107

A WEB OF CEREMONY

The events recounted in myths are used by many native peoples as the basis for rituals which aim to maintain the health and the natural cycles of the earth, people, animals and crops. Native Americans have traditionally believed that a spirit world influences the world of waking consciousness. Sickness or health, starvation or abundance, depend on the proper functioning of the spirits and on their right relationship with humans.

Ritual is performed by many kinds of specialists or holy people, who are known by a variety of names in different languages. Although many Native Americans achieve some communion with spirits through direct experience, such as fasting and obtaining visions, holy people have a special gift for perceiving the working of spirits and knowing how to act upon them to change the world.

Those who concern themselves primarily with healing may most appropriately be referred to as medicine-men or medicine-women. Others use their powers to harm and can be called witches. Most powerful of all are shamans, who are endowed with a high degree of controlling influence over the spirit world. They often exercise this power by undertaking "soul flights" outside their body in order to visit the world of the spirits and negotiate or fight with them on behalf of their clients.

Although the shaman's power is derived from highly personal visions and the ecstatic experience of soul flight, it is always used in the service of the community. Shamans and other holy people assist members of the community through the important stages of their lives as they progress via birth, puberty, maturity and death into the next world. They are vital in maintaining good relations with the spiritual powers that control the weather and the animals on which the community depends for survival.

In many rituals, the shamans of today continue to repeat the feats of mythical heroes as they travel to the sky or to the bottom of the sea to find a patient's missing soul or do battle with monsters and hostile spirits to save their community from famine, disease or disaster. The shaman's mystical experiences are also used to devise responses to new situations. As the tragic history of the Ghost Dance and Sun Dance showed (see pages 126–30), the last one hundred and fifty years have tested this adaptability to the utmost.

Above: A shaman's mask in the shape of a skull. Death and rebirth are common themes in many of the sacred objects used by shamans.

Opposite: This reconstruction of a Chumash rock painting from San Emigdiano, southern California, conveys the visionary experiences that shamans have while in a trance.

Shamans and Medicine

Native American tradition understood the concept of health to include not merely physical and mental well-being, but also such matters as prosperity, harmonious family relationships and lasting friendships.

For Native Americans, good health has traditionally depended on behaving correctly by respecting the spirits of nature and of one's ancestors. Anyone acting in accordance with these rules is assured of well-being, whereas those who transgress against nature invite illness and misfortune. An Iroquois myth about the first medicine man shows the rewards of good conduct. The myth tells how the animals and birds of the forest brought back from the dead a warrior whose honourable behaviour had earned their friendship. After the warrior had been killed in battle and scalped by his enemy, Fox, Bear and Oriole tried to restore him to life by retrieving his scalp. They searched high and low, but without success. Eventually Crow found the scalp laid out to dry in a distant camp. He brought it back, but it was too dry and shrunken to fit back onto the warrior's head. All the other animals then gathered different herbs, leaves and tree bark to make the scalp stick. Eagle gave the precious dew which had accumulated over the years on her back to soften it. Together, they succeeded in bringing the warrior back to life. Fox, Bear and Oriole then revealed to him the secrets of the medicines they had used to revive him and sent him home, where he became the first medicine-man.

However, maintaining good relationships with the animal world is no easy task. In a Cherokee myth, the animals were driven from the forest by the expansion of the human population, and as a result turned against humans, who had formerly lived in harmony with them. In anger, a council was held by every kind of animal, and each devised a disease with which they could afflict human beings. Only the plants remained friendly to humans. Feeling sorry for them, they decided that each of them – be they tree, herb or

Shown in an early 20th-century photograph, an Inuit shaman dons ritual garb to cure a boy of illness. The shaman is wearing a wooden mask and outsize gloves in order to protect himself from malign forces as he tends the sick child.

The Paviotso Curing Ceremony

Atypically, the Paviotso people of the Great Basin conduct quiet, personal healing ceremonies. However noisy or restrained they may be, such rites always focus on a spirit journey by the shaman.

An artist's impression of a Paviotso shaman's vision of how a patient's illness will end positively.

The Paviotso curing rite starts in the evening. The shaman is accompanied by an assistant, who repeats every sentence that he murmurs. The ceremony begins with the shaman stripping to the waist and starting softly to intone a song, which he improvises under the influence of his helping spirits. He is answered by the audience, who join the assistant in repeating each verse. The shaman lights his pipe, takes a few puffs, and hands it around. When he feels ready, he enters a trance and his soul embarks on a journey to discover the cause of the illness and to rescue the patient's soul.

The images that the shaman sees while entranced help him to determine the outcome of the illness. If he sees the patient in a meadow surrounded by living flowers, then the patient will recover; but if the flowers are faded, then he will surely die.

The shaman returns slowly from his long journey. If he has

seen that the illness was caused by a foreign object, he sucks it out of the affected part, either directly through the skin or by using a hollow bone or willow tube. He draws blood and spits it into a hole in the floor, takes a puff of tobacco and dances round the fire. This process is

repeated as often as necessary until he has extracted the object, perhaps a lizard, a worm or a pebble, which he also places in the hole. The rite ends at dawn, with shaman and audience dancing around the fire while magic patterns are painted on the patient's body.

moss – would provide a specific antidote to the diseases imposed by the animals.

Illness is generally thought by Native Americans to have three quite distinct causes, any combination of which may be at the root of a patient's suffering. The first is that a hostile spirit or enemy sorcerer has projected a foreign object into the sick person's body – such as a sharp stone, a splinter, an insect, or a tangled thread. The healing shaman will use divination or clairvoyance to

locate the position of the object, and will then massage or suck the affected area to remove it.

In serious cases, the patient's symptoms may reveal to the shaman that the illness is more deep-seated than a physical malady. In such situations, the patient's soul has left the body, either of its own accord (the second cause of illness), or because it has been stolen by an enemy or lured away by spirits (the third cause). To rescue it, the shaman may have to travel to the underworld, the

The Shaman's Magic Objects

Together with numerous herbs, shamans commonly employ some holy object or substance in order to transform a person's state. Just as a shaman's helping spirits may appear in animal form, these objects are outward signs of an inner spiritual power acquired through the experience of initiation. On the Northwest Coast shamans speak of harbouring a quartz crystal in their bodies, whereas in Northern California they refer to this power more abstractly as a "pain". Such objects and pains can leave the shaman's body and attack others; and, as a result, shamans are often feared as sorcerers.

A shaman's equipment usually includes eagle's feathers, a small bag with crystals and other stones and a rattle or drum. The Apache shaman also uses a magic cord to protect himself against enemies, while among the Haida and Tlingit of the Northwest Coast, the shaman makes himself a full costume with a robe and hat. Shamans from this region also employ various kinds of "soul-catcher"– for example, a tube of hollow bone to scoop up souls flying through the air.

Each of these objects may have a myth explaining its origin and symbolic meaning. For example, the migis shells used in the *midewiwin* ceremony of the Ojibway (see pages 120–21) confer immortality on the initiate because they recall the shell-like hardness of the first humans.

Similarly, the small drum that is now used by dancers in rites invoking the power of the manitou spirits has its origins in a myth. According to this story, the manitous had chosen an old man who was about to die to become a ritual drum. However, as his large body would have made too cumbersome an instrument, the manitous made him fly into pieces when he died, and fashioned one of the pieces into a smaller, more manageable drum. In the

initiation and healing rites that recall this event, the initiate or sick person is symbolically brought to the point of death and said to "fly into pieces" before being reborn into the society or restored to life.

Sacred bundles, also known as medicine bundles, are a vital part of the shaman's equipment. They are among the most revered holy objects, since their contents, and even their external decoration, represent the essential qualities of the deities and spirits. Bundles may be the property of various kinds of group (for example, kinship groups or medicine societies), or belong to an individual, as a memento of a personal encounter with a spirit.

The unwrapping of a sacred bundle is often accompanied by the recitation of myths. The Arapaho recite the myth of the flatpipe bundle over four nights. During the Sun Dance the Kiowa Apache tell the myth of the Ten Grandmothers as they unwrap ten sacred bundles.

Holy objects are not confined to shamans. Plains warriors carried beautifully crafted shields decorated with designs that signified their inner power.

A Tsimshian shaman's rattle from the Nass River on the Northwest Coast. Rattles are used to accompany ritual chanting in healing ceremonies.

These Chumash rock paintings, in the San Emigdiano range of southern California, are thought to have been executed by shamans in a state of ecstatic trance.

sky, or the bottom of the sea (see pages 116–17). The Paviotso believe that if the soul has not gone too far, a shaman can chase after it, but if it has crossed the boundary into the realm of the dead, then it is lost forever. The neighbouring Chumash maintain that one can sometimes see a soul passing on its way to the land of the dead, trailing a blue light behind it, the fatal disease visible as a ball of fire alongside. If one recognizes the person, there may still be time to rush back to the village and give him medicine. But often it is too late and a distant bang is heard as the gate to the land of the dead shuts behind the soul.

Healings are generally communal events. Among the Western Apache, elders would recount myths about the origin of the rite to the assembled community. Then the shaman would sit near the patient and chant throughout the night, invoking the help of Black-Tailed Deer and other spirits. At daybreak, the shaman would dust the patient's head with the pollen from a cat's tail plant.

An entire community may suffer if an individual breaks certain taboos. A hunter who fails to pay proper respect to the soul of an animal he has killed, or a person who excretes near a holy site, may cause an offended spirit to withhold the animals that are the community's main source of food or to inflict a plague upon the village.

Shamanic Initiation

There are a number of different types of shaman, who are known in the many Native languages by a variety of terms. There are also many other kinds of medicine-men, medicine-women, diviners, herbalists and healers. A shaman, who can be either male or female, is a person who is particularly adept at making contact between the world of ordinary people and the spirit world. Only those shamans who have the capacity to enter into a trance while in a state of ecstasy have the power to cure illnesses that have been caused by soul loss. Such shamans, who are prevalent in the hunting societies of the Arctic and sub-Arctic, undertake "soul flights", in which they journey to other realms, either in pursuit of a patient's missing soul or to get advice from the spirits on the whereabouts of game animals.

In order to become a shaman, one must acquire a spiritual power from outside oneself. A person may inherit this, seek it in a quest, or have it imposed upon them by the spirits themselves.

In some regions, especially on the Northwest Coast, shamanic powers are inherited. But inheritance is rarely enough on its own. Among the Haida, a shaman's initial inheritance was followed

113

A photograph of 1908 showing members of a healing society of the
Arikara people of the Plains region carrying rattles used in their sacred
rituals. The name of their society – the Mother Night Men – derives
from their custom of performing nocturnal ceremonies.

by a personal quest. In the southeast, Cherokee shamans could pass on magical spells to their successors, but the actual power to make them work had to be sought by the successors themselves.

In all regions, one of the main means of initiation as a shaman is through dreams. Among the Yurok and Wintu of California and the Paviotso of the Great Basin, a dead shaman may appear in a dream to a descendant, who will then assume the deceased's power. Such visions may come to a person while they are still a child. One Paviotso boy who wanted to become a shaman in order to cure the sick members of his community withdrew to a cave and prayed for the power to heal. Finally overcome by sleep, he had a vision of a healing session, in which a shaman was vainly attempting to revive a patient. The man died and the sleeper

heard the lamentations of his family. Then the rock wall of the cave started to crack open, revealing the figure of a man holding the tail feather of an eagle (a common item in a shaman's sacred bundle). This spirit apparition then taught the boy the art of healing.

Equally, however, shamanic power can come unsought, or even against a person's will. Among the Washo of the Great Basin, people chosen by the spirits to become shamans would be visited by a series of dreams, in which an animal or other spirit appeared and offered teaching. Those who shunned this offer would be plagued with illness until they accepted their destiny, learning in further dreams about secret sites, songs and procedures. Especially among more northerly peoples, involuntary initiation could occur in violent and

Power through Bliss or Terror

Two accounts of involuntary initiation express the conflicting emotions that can affect a person who is chosen by the spirits to become a shaman.

Isaac Tens, a Gitksan shaman, recalled his initiation: "One day when I was cutting wood in the forest, a large owl appeared to me. The owl caught hold of my face and tried to lift me up. I lost consciousness. When I came to, I found myself lying in the snow, covered with ice and blood. All the way home, the trees seemed to shake and lean over me; tall trees were crawling after me as if they had been snakes. When I got home I felt very cold and fell into a trance. I felt that flies were completely covering my face, and then that I was caught up in a huge whirlpool. Two shamans were brought to treat me. They said that it was time for me to train as a shaman too. But at that time I took no notice."

"Another time I went hunting and shot an owl. But when I went to pick it up, there was nothing there, not even a feather. Then at my fishing camp I heard a hubbub of voices, even though it was deserted. I ran away and the voices pursued me. When I looked round, there was still no-one there and I again fell into a trance. My father and some shamans tried to help me but my flesh seemed

A heart-shaped Tsimshian charm from the Northwest Coast contains the effigy of an owl. In Native American myth, the figure of the owl is frequently associated with the afterlife.

to be boiling. My body was quivering and I started to sing. These chants didn't come from me, but from the spirit. Then I saw many birds and animals, which no-one else there could see. Gradually I memorized the songs by repeating them."

Though terrifying, shamanic initiation can also be blissful. The Iglulik shaman Aua recalled: "I would sometimes start weeping, without knowing why. Then suddenly, for no good reason, I would be filled with a great, inexplicable delight ... in the midst of such a mysterious and overwhelming joy, I became a shaman. I could hear and see in a totally different way. I had gained the shaman-light in my brain and body, and could see through the darkness of life. This light wasn't visible to other people, but it shone out from me to the spirits of earth and sky and sea. They could see it, and they became my helping spirits."

extraordinary ways. An Iglulik Inuit woman called Uvavnuk went outside one winter night and was struck by a huge ball of lightning which entered her body. Before falling unconscious, she felt inwardly illuminated by a spirit that was half human, half polar bear. Presently, she regained consciousness and, enthused by the spirit inside her, went on to become a great shaman.

Along the Northwest Coast too, shamanic initiation was often extremely violent. Nootka

shamans would spend years preparing for their first encounter with a spirit, but even so when the meeting took place they might collapse with blood trickling from mouth, nose and ears, or even drop dead on the spot. In the same region, Kwakiutl or Tsimshian shamans might struggle to master or even "kill" the spirit in order to acquire its power. In this way, each shaman repeated the original cosmic battles of the heroes of myth in their own personal experience.

Soul Flights, Dreams and Vision Quests

Many Native myths concern the exploits of archetypal heroic figures. Such legends are constantly being re-enacted, and in the process reinforced, in the contemporary experiences of shamans. These may take the form of soul flights, dreams or visions.

Shamans who embark on soul flights to rescue people's souls are often repeating the journeys of mythical heroes. One such archetypal figure is the husband who journeys to the underworld to reclaim his wife, which is the subject of many Native myths, and recalls the Greek legend of Orpheus and Eurydice. Another myth tells how a Bella Coola shaman on the Northwest Coast succeeded in rescuing his son from the ocean by lowering a rope from his canoe, even though the son had already been reduced to a skeleton by the waves.

Such myths are recounted whenever a shaman sets out to bring back the soul of a dying patient. The battles that he must fight on the way against monsters and hostile spirits may be a re-enactment of the struggles that he fought during his initiation. Among the Coast Salish, several shamans may collaborate in retrieving a sick patient's lost guardian animal spirit. Assembling at night, the shamans form themselves into the shape of a canoe. To the accompaniment of drums and rattles, each shaman mimes the action of paddling and sings the song of his own guardian spirit as his soul descends into the bowels of the earth.

Until well into the twentieth century, shamans of the Iglulik Inuit would observe an especially

Newitti, a Kwakiutl village on Vancouver Island, British Columbia, photographed in 1881. Shamanism was particularly strong among peoples of the Northwest Coast region.

The Woman of the Sea

The myth of The Woman of the Sea – sometimes called Sedna ("The Great Food Dish") – relates how the Inuit were provided with plentiful fish and animals.

This drawing by an Inuit shaman shows Takanakapsaluk leading the sea creatures that grew from her severed fingers.

A common myth among the Inuit tells of the Woman of the Sea, or Mistress of the Animals. Known in different regions as Sedna or Takanakapsaluk, she married a fulmar against her parents' wishes. Later, she became disillusioned with her husband and ran away. Her parents rescued her, but when the angry fulmar found their little kayak on the water, he raised a fierce storm by beating his wings. Realizing that the kayak was about to capsize, the girl's parents started blaming her for their misfortune and told her to cast herself into the sea. Despite her protestations of innocence and her screams for mercy, her parents threw her overboard. As she clung desperately onto the gunwale, her father took his knife and, one by one, cut off all her fingers.

When the fulmar saw that the girl was drowned, he allowed

the storm to subside and let her parents proceed safely home. As the girl sank to the sea bed, her fingers came back to life as sea creatures – for example as a fish, a seal, a whale and a walrus.

It was thus through Sedna's suffering that animals crucial to the Inuit's survival came into being. Together they provide meat, blubber for heating and

lighting in the long dark winters and skins for protective clothing. However, humanity's sins accumulate as filth in Sedna's hair, and having no fingers she cannot comb it clean again. When her hair gets dirty, her anger causes epidemics or storms, or makes her withhold the seals and other animals on which the people depend.

perilous ritual whenever their community was threatened by famine. As the source of this misfortune was always the Woman of the Sea, a strong and brave shaman was delegated to dive to the ocean floor and appease her by combing her hair. His preparation for this dangerous task involved gathering the tribe together in his house. Here he would sit for a long time in silence and breathing deeply, naked except for fur boots and mittens, and separated from his people by a curtain. He then began to call for help from his guiding spirits. After gaining the spirits' permission to

descend, the shaman would slide down a passage that had opened up in the ice beneath the house, leading directly to the bottom of the sea. After his departure the audience remained in silence.

Meanwhile, the shaman had to negotiate a series of deadly obstacles on the sea bed, including three large rolling stones that tried to crush him. Entering the Sea Woman's house, he found her sulking next to a pool containing the creatures which she refused to release into the sea. Her long hair hung over her eyes, clogged into a filthy tangle by the sins of humankind. The shaman

This shield belonged to the famous Oglala Sioux warrior Crazy Horse. His name is derived from a vision that he once experienced involving a bucking horse. This supernatural encounter later helped him to become an illustrious fighter.

would carefully place his hand on her shoulder, turning her face towards the light, and begin the delicate task of combing the matted hair out of her eyes. As he did so, he spoke to her in the special language of the spirits, saying: "Those above can no longer help the seals up by grasping their fore-flippers." She would reply, "The secret sins and the breaches of taboo bar the way for the animals." As she grew calmer, she picked up the animals one by one and dropped them into a current that flowed through her house into the open sea. A good supply of meat was now assured.

Having appeased her, the shaman began his return journey. The community heard him approaching from afar. Finally, with a loud cry, he shot up into the house behind the curtain, gasping for breath. Intense silence ensued for a moment, before the shaman announced: "Words will arise." Then, one by one, those present began to confess the misdeeds that weighed on their consciences.

Dreams and Visions

Many native traditions regard the shaman's soul journey as a specialized form of the experiences that every layperson has in their dreams. While everyone's soul has the capacity to wander in their sleep, a shaman's soul travels in a more purposeful way. Dreaming is seen as happening in a realm that is inseparable from everyday life. For example, the Zuni of the Southwest regard dreams as having a bearing on real events. An action in a dream is not considered complete until its counterpart has taken place in waking life, and many crucial actions are based on a preceding dream. People thus try to influence events. After receiving a good dream, they tell no-one until it has been fulfilled; on the other hand, a bad dream is shared, in the hope of forestalling its fulfilment.

Native Americans make no rigid distinction between dreams and waking visions. So widespread is the quest for a vision that it may be regarded as the most distinctive common element of Native religions. Among the Plains peoples, for example, everyone sought a vision at least once in their lifetime, while many undertook regular vision quests. The vision that the quest revealed endowed the individual seeker with personal power, while the tribe's visions taken as a whole added to its communal store of spiritual power.

On the Northwest Coast, laypersons would often undertake terrifying vision quests. Some Nootka vision-seekers died of exposure, while among the Coast Salish, seekers would weigh themselves down with rocks and plunge into deep water. Children who were afraid to take part in such quests were beaten and deprived of food.

Great shamans and war leaders on the Plains had visions that affected the entire community. The renowned Oglala Sioux warrior Crazy Horse gained his name from one such momentous vision, in which the horse he was riding through an ethereal spirit landscape began to prance about erratically. Another vision warned Crazy Horse always to stay mounted if he wished to remain invincible. Thus reassured, he became a fearless fighter. True to the vision's warning, he finally met his death while dismounted.

The Plains peoples see the vision quest as a form of prayer (known to the Sioux as a "lamentation") that lies at the very heart of their way of life. In the lamentation, a person stands humble and powerless before the "Great Mystery", Wakan Tanka. Visions are sought under the guidance of experienced elders, and recounted to them afterwards for interpretation. The aim of the quest is not to enter the state of ecstasy attained by the shamans of the Arctic and sub-Arctic, but to gain a clear insight into the future.

The vision thus plays a central role in Plains culture, forming the basis of most rituals (such as the Sun Dance), and giving guidance in times of traumatic change. The story of the nineteenth-century Sioux healer Black Elk illustrates this.

At the age of five, Black Elk had a vision, in which two men flew swiftly towards him out of a cloud, singing with voices of thunder. Four years later voices came to him in another vision, saying, "It is time! Your Grandfathers are calling you!" The two men from the earlier vision then appeared, and took him into a heaven full of dancing horses. They passed through a door in a rainbow and met the spirits of the Sky, of the Earth and of the Four Directions, who each bestowed their special gifts on him. Looking at the spirit of the Earth, the young Black Elk recognized himself as an old man. From a high vantage point on a mountain top, he then saw the Sioux nation's sacred hoop broken and a holy tree devoid of birds, representing the people's future desolation. However, suddenly the tree blossomed again and a powerful song swept over him. Later, as his people were persecuted and their buffalo herds massacred, Black Elk clung to this vision. Until the final massacre of the Sioux at Wounded Knee in December 1890, the Ghost Dance (see pages 130–31) seemed to herald the salvation promised in his vision. In old age, Black Elk looked back on his life regretfully as "the story of a mighty vision given to a man too weak to use it … and of a people's dream that ended in bloody snow".

This talisman, made from a golden eagle, was carried by a Plains warrior, and would have been one of the most sacred items in his medicine bundle.

Sacred Societies

Some Native American cultures do not have individual shamans but instead collectivize the role of the holy man into sacred societies based upon a common ideal or ritual. These societies are of various kinds, but their activities commonly focus on rites of passage, celebrations of natural fertility and healing ceremonies.

One of the most significant rites of passage marked by Native American peoples is that of puberty. This phase in the human life-cycle has several rites associated with it, many of which concern the individual's acquisition of spiritual power. Thus, a widespread practice is for adolescent children – both male and female – to engage in a vision quest. In addition, some cultures deem it essential to segregate girls from the rest of the community during their first menstruation, since their menstrual blood is believed to contain dangerous spiritual properties. The Lakota Sioux regard this enforced isolation as having the same purifying function for girls that a sweat lodge has for adolescent boys.

Many peoples lay particular emphasis on the fact that puberty signals the full integration of an individual into the community. In such communities, the central event in a person's transition into adulthood is a public ceremony conducted by a sacred society. For example, the puberty rite of passage is one of several communal rituals celebrated by the Kachina Society of the farming Pueblo peoples (see page 121).

These wood and leather articulated puppets depicting a family of ghosts were used in initiation rites by the Kwakiutl people of the Northwest Coast.

Societies of healers developed among the farming peoples of the Northeast. There existed among the Huron several such groups, each specializing in curing a particular disease. They ritually enacted the killing and resurrection of their members, in order to endow them with the power to heal. Another healing society, the Iroquois "False Face", was named after a giant who challenged the Creator to a contest to move a mountain. In the ensuing struggle, the mountain toppled into the giant's face, disfiguring it permanently. Defeated, the giant agreed to dedicate himself to healing humans. As a consequence, members of this society wear masks representing the giant's twisted features as they tend the sick.

Women's societies were prevalent in the upper Missouri region. Among the Mandan, the Goose Women and those belonging to the Society of the White Buffalo Cow performed rites to attract buffalo herds to their territories and to ensure a plentiful corn harvest.

There were also a number of secret societies – for example, the Cannibal Society of the Kwakiutl, whose induction ceremony was believed to involve eating parts of a corpse.

The link between ceremony and myth is evident from

A Celebration of Rain

*In the Pueblo villages of the Hopi, initiates of the Kachina Society dance at ceremonies that mark seasonal changes. One particularly elaborate rite celebrates the arrival of the winter rains, which the Hopi believe are brought to them by the **kachinas** – the spirit essences of all life on earth.*

The farming Pueblo peoples of the Southwest believe that the rain-bringing *kachina* spirits descend in winter from the cloud-topped San Francisco Peaks to spend six months in their villages.

To mark this crucial event in the crop-growing cycle, the Hopi hold a mid-winter ceremony known as the *powamu,* or bean dance. *Powamu* celebrates the germination and growth of such staple crops as beans and corn, and is also used to initiate children into the *kachina* cult.

The 16-day-long festival begins with the planting of seeds in beds of moist sand inside a steamy *kiva*, a sacred underground chamber specially prepared for the occasion. Dances then begin, led by men dressed as the *kachina* spirits. Once the seeds have sprouted, they are used in a performance by carved puppets that mimic the dancers. Against a painted backdrop of rain and lightning, marionettes depicting water serpents chase away the sun, to forestall the premature arrival of the summer drought. Other puppets then grind corn meal, which is sprinkled by masked clowns on to the heads of initiates. On the final day of *powamu*, the new crop of beansprouts is harvested and carried through the village.

Although the *kachina* bring rain, a vital element of life on Earth, their home is the Land of the Dead.

Zuni women in the arid Southwest sow their crops in "waffle gardens" – beds of soil subdivided into small compartments to minimize evaporation. The Zuni, like the other farming peoples of this region, celebrate the various stages of the crop-growing cycle in a number of annual festivals.

the initiation ritual conducted by the *midewiwin*, or Great Medicine Society, of the Ojibway and Chippewa of the Great Lakes region. A creation myth of these peoples relates how the first humans were made by the spirits – chief among them Manitou – and were intended to live forever, through regeneration every hundred years. The Ojibway trickster Manabozho, who was present at the creation, watched as Manitou fashioned human figures out of clay, put a hard migis shell on their heads (signifying the durability of their existence) and then brought them to life.

Human immortality immediately came under threat when one spirit, jealous at not being involved in the creation, opened up a direct route from the human world to the realm of death. However, Manitou subsequently taught Manabozho how, through ritual observance, he might sacrifice himself and be reborn. The *midewiwin* ceremony recalls this feat. Candidates for initiation into the society, or sick patients, are symbolically killed and then revived, with migis shells placed on their bodies to act as points of entry for Manitou's power.

Hunting Ceremonies

While some peoples, particularly in the Northeast, Southeast and Southwest, developed sophisticated systems of agriculture, others relied heavily on the traditional method of acquiring food – hunting. This required great care and scrupulous observance of custom: not only were animals seen as sentient beings like humans, but they were also believed to be able to change into humans, and vice versa.

The fluid boundaries between the human and animal worlds could be used to advantage by shamans in their retrieval of souls. An Inupiat legend from northern Alaska recounts how a man was walking along the beach when his soul was abducted by a boat full of spirits and turned into a whale. His body lay where it had fallen for the entire winter. In spring, when the whales migrated past his village, his soul returned to his body and he regained consciousness. This experience marked the man's initiation as a shaman. The insight he gained from having lived among the whales as one of their number enabled him to

Photographed in 1915, ceremonial dancers of the Kwakiutl Hamatsa Society wear many different masks symbolizing animal spirits. The dancers in long-beaked masks represent Hokhokw, a creature that cracks open people's skulls and eats their brains.

persuade them to let themselves be hunted by members of his village. He starved an enemy village into submission by asking the whales to disappear from its hunting grounds.

Sometimes, a hunter's skill derived from having had a close kinship with an animal. A myth of the Mistassini Cree of Quebec tells how a bear adopted a boy and shared with him its diet of porcupine, beaver and partridge. At the approach of winter, they prepared to hibernate in the bear's lair. However, the bear suddenly heard the boy's father singing far away, in an effort to locate his lost son. Although the bear tried to drown the sound out with its own song, the father's voice proved too powerful. As winter progressed, the boy's father sang again, only this time closer at hand – he was evidently approaching the lair in search of his son. The bear attempted to distract the hunter by hurling into his path various live prey animals that it had hoarded in its lair. Though it tried this ruse several times, it failed to deflect the father from his purpose. In desperation to avoid being located and killed by the vengeful father, the bear lay on its back with its legs in the air and tried to raise a violent storm, but all to no avail.

Finally, realizing that it could not halt the father's relentless advance, the bear bit off one of its forelegs and gave it to the boy as a memento, exhorting him to keep it safely. At that moment, the hunter broke into the lair and killed the bear. The boy was taken home by his father and grew up to be a successful hunter, with a special understanding of the ways of bears. His skill allowed him to feed his people from his own kills, and he was always able to find bears for other hunters.

Native Americans believe that all creatures are under the control of a guardian spirit, a Master or Mistress of the Animals. This figure is understood either literally, as the father or mother of every animal in a particular species, or figuratively, as the species' collective spirit, comprising the souls of all its individuals. Occasionally, the guiding spirit may take the form of a gigantic animal, such as the beaver spirit that is believed by the Montagnais of Quebec to be as big as a hut;

This Inuit wooden carving of a whale was attached to the bow of a hunting canoe in order to attract and assuage the guardian spirit of the whales. Respect towards the animals hunted was regarded as essential.

other peoples, such as the Mistassini Cree, refer to animals as the guardian spirit's "pets".

It was widely thought that animals and their spirit owners sacrificed themselves willingly to hunters who accorded them the proper "respect". However, this was far from straightforward, since correct hunting behaviour was fraught with taboos. For example, the Western Apache considered it a grave offence against the Deer Spirit to boil a deer's stomach or eat its tongue. The Cherokee claimed that when a hunter shot a deer, the chief Deer Spirit asked the dying animal whether it had heard the hunter pray for pardon. If not, the Chief Deer would track the hunter to his tent and cripple him with rheumatism. Hunters who did not know the appropriate prayer had to protect themselves from pursuit by building a fire on the path behind them.

Many peoples believed that an individual or clan could form a special relationship with a particular species, which then acted as their guardian animal. The Iroquois referred to the animal patron of a clan as a "totem", and proscribed the hunting of this species. The convention was also widely observed on the Plains, but among Great Basin peoples hunting was allowed if the person meant to assimilate the power of the guardian animal. In many areas of North America it was the practice to dress up like the animal patron, wear its mask, or keep parts of its body in a sacred bundle.

In respecting an animal, the hunter effectively treated it as a person. In a myth of the Thompson (Ntlakyapamuk) Indians, a hunter lost sight of two female goats he was chasing, then encountered them again in the form of two human women. He married them, but they refused to have sexual intercourse with him until they came into season. When he was about to return to his

123

own people, the goats assured him that he would be a successful goat hunter, provided that he treated the bodies of killed goats with the respect that he would accord people. He was not to kill the females, for they were his wives. Neither should he kill the kids, for they might be his own children. He was allowed to shoot only the adult males, his brothers-in-law. However, he need feel no sorrow, since in perishing they would only be relinquishing the goat part of their being, while the human part of them would return home alive.

Careful disposal of bones was another important way of honouring an animal one had killed. They were often rearranged into complete skeletons, with great care being taken not to mislay a single bone. This ensured that, although the animal had been eaten, it would still be reborn. Bear bones were treated with particular respect.

In seasonal rites, one animal could represent the entire catch. An important ritual of the Hupa of northwestern California marked the catching of the season's first migrating salmon. In preparation, a fire (representing the creation) was lit inside a

This *Inukshuk* – a heap of stones assembled in the shape of a human being – was erected by the Iglulik Inuit of northern Canada to direct the migration of caribou.

sweat lodge, which symbolized the cosmos. The first fish caught was cooked over the fire, eaten, and its remains disposed of with great ceremony.

There were many other ways in which hunters and their communities could display humility towards animals and avoid offending a species or its guardian. Inuit women butchering a seal on the shore would customarily throw a kidney or bladder back into the water, as a token of thanks and as a votive offering to ward off future shortage. Similarly, hunters were not allowed to boast of their prowess or reveal their intent to kill an animal before a hunt. One Zuni legend concerns a woman who dreamt that a deer offered itself to her. She did not tell her husband her dream, contenting herself with a vaguely expressed hope that he might have good luck while hunting. Although she was certain that the hunt would be successful, she dared not say so. Equally, her husband may have guessed the content of her dream, but could not ask her to divulge it.

Some hunting societies, such as the peoples of the Plains and the Great Lakes, used the image of the Happy Hunting Ground to express their concept of an afterlife as a reward for good conduct. A myth of the Seneca shows how this realm provided moral lessons. A trickster called Mischief-Maker constantly angered his people with his practical jokes. One day, he was borne aloft on a column of smoke and set down in a land of beautiful people, with fields full of beans and pumpkins and tents stacked with deer and bear meat. After living happily there for a hundred years, he was sent back to his people by the chief of the realm, with instructions to tell them what he had seen. He changed his name from Mischief-Maker to Peace-Maker and told the Seneca that the Great Spirit would guide and protect them if they led righteous lives and shunned evil: "There are spirits in the pumpkin and in the bean, spirits in the water, the fire and all the trees and berries. Remember to thank the Great Spirit for these, throw tobacco in the fire as an offering, and after your death you will live forever, hunting and fishing in the Happy Hunting Ground."

Hunters who Married Animal Girls

The union of a mythical hunter with the daughter of the spirit "owner" or "master" of an animal species is the subject of many Native American myths. Two stories from very diferent areas show how such marriages are the ultimate confirmation of a harmonious relationship between a hunting people and the animals that form its main source of food.

In a myth of the Mistassini Cree of Quebec, a hunter married a caribou girl and learned to see reality from the caribous' perspective. Whereas other hunters, when shooting a caribou, simply saw the animal fall down and die, he could see its spirit still running away, while its carcass remained behind in the form of a white cape.

A Pawnee myth tells how a young hunter was about to kill a young female buffalo at a watering hole when she suddenly revealed herself as a beautiful young woman. He instantly fell in love with her and gave her a necklace of blue and white beads. They married and set up camp together.

One day the hunter returned to find his wife and camp gone. He searched in vain, finally returning in great sorrow to his tribe. Later, he met a small boy wearing the same necklace of blue and white beads. The boy, whom he recognized as his son by his buffalo wife, led him back to the land of the buffaloes. The bulls were initially suspicious and, before allowing him to join the herd, challenged him to perform several difficult tasks, including identifying his own wife among the cows.

Once the hunter had passed all the tests, the buffaloes

This Shoshoni hide painting depicts a dance after a successful buffalo hunt. Peoples of the Plains believed that they had special links with this vital animal.

accepted him. He took his wife back to meet his own people, but found them starving. The buffaloes agreed to help by allowing the Pawnees to hunt them. The hunter's son joined them in the form of a yellow calf, which the hunter warned the humans never to harm, or there would be nobody to guide the herd to them each year. But

the son said, "No, sacrifice me to the Great Spirit Tirawa Atius. A new calf will take my place each year. Tan my hide and use it to wrap a sacred bundle containing an ear of corn and a piece of meat. Every hungry season, call upon the calf to lead the herd back to the people, and add a piece of the new season's meat to the bundle."

The Sun Dance

The Sun Dance celebration of the Earth's renewal was held at the beginning of summer by many peoples on the Plains and in the Northeast. While the Sioux performed the rite annually, some other peoples such as the Blackfeet repeated it only every two or three years. Each people placed a different emphasis on the dance, explained in different myths.

The Sun Dance was a grand public spectacle, involving fasting, banquets, communal games, and healing sessions. It could last for up to two weeks. Participants would implore the spirits to give them and their families protection. Among peoples of the Great Sioux Nation, the central feature of the dance was a four-day period in which young braves gained spiritual power both for themselves and for their tribe by dancing with their skin pierced by wooden skewers. These were embedded in the warrior's chest, back or shoulders and fastened to a central pole by leather thongs. Each man would dance for hours around the pole, leaning outwards to put the maximum strain on the skewers until they ripped his flesh and he fell to the ground in a trance. Some devotees also used the skewers to drag heavy buffalo skulls around the camp circle. Warriors would stand or dance for hours, or even days, staring into the sun. Participants in the ritual gained great prestige, especially among the Sioux, and warriors from the Oglala tribe would display their Sun Dance scars proudly for the rest of their lives.

This headdress was worn by the virtuous figure of Feather Woman in the Blackfoot Sun Dance. The Blackfoot people trace the origin of the ceremony to Feather Woman's love for Morning Star.

Although the Sun Dance was traditionally held to ensure the fertility of the buffalo herd and success in warfare, its significance was not confined to hunting or battle. Rather, the ritual lay at the very heart of religious observance, as a form of prayer in which a person offered himself up as a sacrifice for the renewal of the world. Mortification of the flesh was central to the ritual, especially on the Plains, as it signified humility before the Great Spirit, stressing that the only thing that a person had to give was his body.

Historical evidence suggests that the Sun Dance evolved slowly. Like the *midewiwin* ritual of the Ojibway or the Medicine Rite of the Winnebago, it may have developed as an assertion of tribal solidarity in response to two centuries of European aggression. Its origins and form are explained in a rich body of myths.

One of these, from the Blackfoot, gives the dance a celestial origin. A young girl called Feather Woman was sleeping out of doors in the summer and woke before dawn. She was captivated by the beauty of the Morning Star, who was a young man. Morning Star returned her love, and together they climbed into the sky on a thread from a spider's web. Morning Star's mother, the Moon, and his father, the Sun, welcomed Feather Woman. For a long while, she lived happily in the sky with her husband, and she bore him a son, Star Boy.

One day, Feather Woman's mother-in-law gave her a tool for harvesting roots, but warned her that she should on no account dig up a large turnip that was growing nearby. However, overcome by curiosity, she eventually uprooted the vegetable. The turnip turned out to be the plug closing the hole through which she had ascended into heaven – seen from the earth, it appeared in the sky as the Pole Star. Looking down, she saw her own village far below and was overcome by homesickness. When the Sun came home and saw what she had done, he angrily told her to leave. Morning Star gave her a parting gift of a sacred hat and an elk-skin robe, clothes that could be worn only by a pure woman, and with great sadness let her and her son down through the hole.

Shortly afterwards, Feather Woman died, leaving Star Boy an impoverished orphan. He was taunted by the other children, and later spurned by the woman he loved, because of a mysterious scar on his face. One day he learned from an old female shaman that the blemish had been made by his grandfather the Sun, and he was consumed by a desire to visit him. He waited on the shore of the western ocean until sunset, when across the water a shaft of light appeared, and upon this he

travelled to the Sun. Although the Sun was initially displeased to see him, he later relented and said to him, "Go back to the Blackfeet and tell them that I will heal their sick if they hold an annual festival in my honour." Star Boy duly returned to earth and passed on the Sun's instructions for performing the dance. In memory of Feather Woman, the Blackfeet believe that the Sun Dance must be initiated by a virtuous woman.

The Cheyenne stage a similar dance, but base it on a different myth. This legend tells how they were suffering a great famine. Crops withered and animals died. To seek help, a young man known as Rustling Corn decided to go on a pilgrimage to a distant sacred mountain. He secretly persuaded the chief's beautiful wife to accompany him, but was careful to abstain from sexual intercourse with her until they had safely completed their mission and were on the return journey. On the

In this painting of a Cheyenne Sun Dance ceremony, a dancer
hangs by rawhide thongs from the tree at the centre of the lodge.
Bison skulls attached to his back add to his weight.

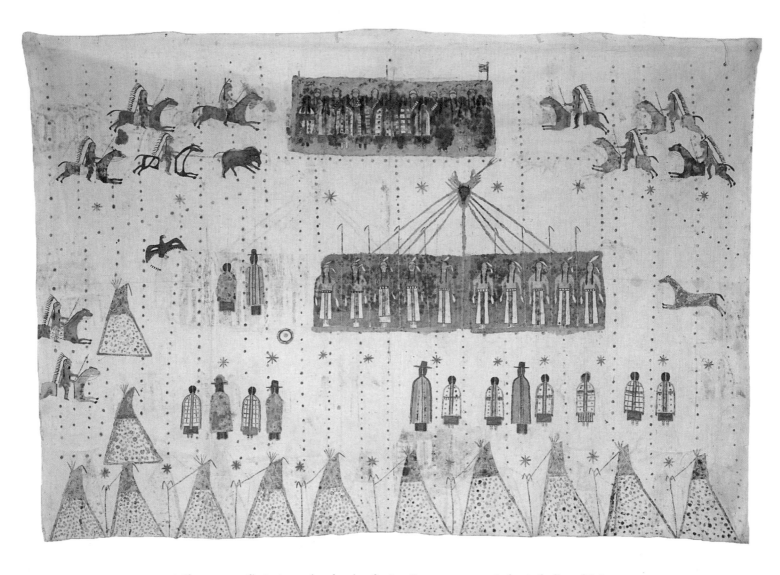

A Cheyenne muslin tent covering showing the Sun Dance ceremony. In front of a line of tipis, women and children are pictured as they observe the ritual. Under a canopy specially erected for the purpose around a central tree, participants are seen assembled for the dance.

mountain, they were received by the Thunder Spirit and the god Mayun, who gave them detailed instructions about how to perform the Sun Dance. Mayun gave Rustling Corn a cap of buffalo skin with two horns and renamed him Upright Horns ("Tomtivsi"). Mayun told him, "Follow my instructions accurately, and then, when you depart from here, all of the heavenly bodies will move. Roaring Thunder will awaken, the sun, moon, stars and the rain will bring forth fruits of all kinds… Take this horned cap to wear when you perform the ceremony that I have bestowed on you, and you will control the buffalo and all other animals."

The pilgrims returned home and as they did so, the Earth sprang to life again. Upright Horns instructed the Cheyenne in the ritual of the dance, and the sacred buffalo-skin cap was handed down to all future generations.

Every major element of this myth is reenacted in the way the Cheyenne perform the Sun Dance. The pledge to hold the ceremony is often made by a person or community in distress, as in the original famine. The pledger's wife represents the mythical companion of Upright Horns, and the couple must refrain from sex until the dance is over. Priests officiating at the ritual, themselves

White Buffalo Woman

Plains peoples looked upon the buffalo as an intermediary with the Creator. According to the Sioux, it was a buffalo in human form that brought them many important rites, including the Sun Dance.

A myth of the Lakota Sioux tells how the supreme spirit, Wakan Tanka ("Great Mystery"), once sent as an emissary a beautiful woman clad in a white dress.

The woman brought with her a two-piece pipe, which she gave to the Sioux as a sacred object, explaining that, once assembled, it represented the entire universe. Its circular stone bowl signified the Earth and all its creatures, while the wooden stem, rising from the centre of the bowl, indicated a direct link between the Earth and the sky. Its smoke also performed a dual function, both carrying prayers to the spirit ancestors as it drifted upwards and imparting strength to the smokers of the pipe. After she had given the Sioux the pipe, the woman transformed herself into a white buffalo calf and disappeared.

Along with the sacred pipe, White Buffalo Woman also imparted to the Sioux seven rites that are central to their religion. These included the vision quest, the rites of purification in the sweat lodge, funeral rites that ensure that the soul of the deceased returns to the Great Spirit instead of wandering the Earth as a ghost, puberty rites for girls and the Sun Dance.

However, another legend places the origin of the Sun Dance much later than the other rites. According to this account, the ritual was introduced because the Sioux had become negligent in their respect for the sacred pipe. A man called Kablaya received a vision referring to a new form of prayer that would help to restore the strength and the faith of the people. This was the Sun Dance.

A page from the historical record ("Winter Count") of the Brulé Sioux shows White Buffalo Woman inside a circle of tipis. The sacred pipe is depicted immediately above the animal.

former pledgers, represent Mayun and the Thunder Spirit. The participants are collectively referred to as "the ones who bring back to life".

In the nineteenth century, along with the rest of Plains culture, the Sun Dance came under threat from white settlement. The US Government saw it as a focus of resistance, especially among the Sioux, and outlawed it in 1881. This was a devastating blow for the Indians, for, without the Sun Dance, they thought that the world would not renew itself. Some Indians therefore continued to perform it in secret, while others turned to another ritual, the Ghost Dance (see page 130). When this

in turn was suppressed in 1890, Shoshoni and Ute shamans, guided by dreams, shifted the focus of the Sun Dance towards healing.

Other peoples performed a sanitized version of the dance for tourists, wearing harnesses instead of piercing their flesh. The Indian Reorganization Act of 1934 revoked the ban on piercing, and eventually led to a large-scale revival in the 1960s, as Native Americans began to reassert their cultural identity. The Sun Dance is now widespread, and has become a major religious event. It is currently attracting many adherents away from the Native American Church (see pages 130–31).

Rituals and Cults

A long series of Native religious revivals arose in response to European encroachment, starting in the east in the seventeenth century. These movements had a strong moral dimension, which interpreted Indians' suffering as a punishment for unethical conduct, and held out the hope of renewed happiness through repentance.

Revival movements could take the form either of peaceful separatism or of violent confrontation. One of the most enduring of the peaceful sects was the *Gaiwiio* ("Good Word") movement, founded in 1799 by the Seneca medicine man Handsome Lake. *Gaiwiio* called for a return to traditional ways, using the Christian form of preaching to deliver its message. Other movements were violently anti-white, such as the armed insurrection led by the Shawnee prophet Lalawethika in 1805.

In 1889–90, the desperate plight of the peoples of the Great Basin and the Plains, caused by white expansion, led many to participate in the Ghost Dance. This messianic movement was led by Wovoka, a Paiute holy man who had experienced a vision in which the Great Spirit told him that if Indians devoted themselves to tireless dancing, their ancestors ("ghosts") would return to usher in a renewed era of peace and plenty. As Wovoka's message spread, groups of devotees danced for days on end, often collapsing from exhaustion.

Wovoka's movement began peacefully, but turned violent when it spread into the neighbouring Plains region, with its proud warrior tradition. Many people were attracted by promises of a return of the buffalo herds and the expulsion of the whites. The movement ended tragically in December 1890, when US troops massacred a

This Pawnee Ghost Dance drum (*c*.1890) is decorated with an image of the Thunderbird, a spirit that was invoked during the ritual.

Lakota Sioux encampment at Wounded Knee in South Dakota. Earlier in the same month, the Hunkpapa Sioux chief Sitting Bull was killed by Native police during his arrest for supporting the Ghost Dance (see page 101).

Despite the demise of the Ghost Dance, the establishment of reservations at this time brought diverse Native groups together and fostered the spread of other pan-Indian movements. The most important of these was the peyote cult, which began in Mexico in the 1880s. This cult encouraged the use of peyote, a cactus containing the hallucinogenic drug mescaline. Peyotism contained a mixture of Native and Christian elements. Its hybrid nature, together with the fact that it made visions accessible to anyone without disciplined ritual, antagonized traditionalists. Yet the cult, renamed the Native American Church in 1918, continued to flourish, especially in the Midwest and Southeast.

The legends associated with peyotism reflect its controversial nature. Adherents of the cult identify the cactus with a myth prophesying that the Navajo will find a plant more powerful than any of their existing medicines. However, Navajo opposed to the Native American Church link peyote with the myth of the "Great Gambler of Pueblo Bonito", who used the plant to trick the original inhabitants of the pueblo – the Snake People – out of their women, their land and even their lives.

A Ghost Dance shirt. Dancers believed that such garments were imbued with magical properties that would protect them from bullets. The massacre at Wounded Knee in 1890 showed their faith to be tragically misplaced.

THE ALIEN EYE

From the earliest years of European exploration in North America, artist-explorers recorded the appearance, habitats and customs of indigenous peoples. However different their style and content, the images they produced, from the sixteenth century onwards, all display a high regard for their subjects and show the artists' commitment to render realistically the new world they encountered. Everything was of interest: styles of dwelling, tribal distinctions, and methods of hunting and fishing. These early records provide us with a view of Native Americans before their cultures and beliefs were seriously affected by the influence of whites.

The towne of Pomeiock and true forme of their howses, couered and enclosed some wth matts, and some wth barcks of trees. All compassed abowt wth smale poles stock thick together in stedd of a wall.

3

Above: John White, who visited America in 1586, was one of the earliest British artist-explorers to document Native American life. This watercolour of the village of Pomeiooc, Virginia, was one of twenty-three produced for a book for Sir Walter Raleigh.

The manner of their fishing.

People of North Carolina fishing with spears, nets and fish traps in a watercolour of 1587 by John White (left). The copperplate (below) of a Native Virginian is taken from *Hollar's Foreign Portraits* by Wenceslas Hollar (1607–77).

Expansion westwards by whites from the 17th to the late 19th century brought artists into contact with new ways of life. A Dakota woman and Assiniboine child are depicted in Karl Bodmer's *Travels into the Interior of North America, 1832–34* (above left), while J. Verelest's 18th-century painting shows the proud and impressive King of the Maguas, Sa Ga Yeath Qua Pieth Ton (left).

Right: These highly decorated war canoes belong to the Makah of the Northwest Coast. The artist, Paul Kane (1810–71), produced many such studies of tribal life in Canada for the Hudson Bay Company.

THE NATIVE AMERICAN LEGACY

In a continent dominated by newcomers, Native American peoples have an ancient and distinctive view of the relationship between human beings and the Earth they inhabit, and of the continuity between past, present and future generations. After decades of being ignored or suppressed, Native culture has experienced a resurgence since the 1960s. Its proponents argue that the ancestral wisdom it embodies has much to teach modern society.

A common thread running through Native American attitudes to the natural environment is that the Earth, which existed long before the advent of humans, possesses a consciousness of its own. Every living person is believed to gain a sense of belonging and historical continuity by learning about their specific locality, the place where their ancestors lived and died. A modern Western Apache elder has expressed this affinity in the following terms: "The land looks after us. The land keeps badness away." Past and present are linked by the constant narration of events that took place in particular locations. Communal myths about how the world came to exist in its present form, stories about one's own ancestors

and personal recollections from one's own lifetime all contribute to this body of wisdom. As the contemporary Pueblo writer Leslie Marmon Silko has said, it sometimes seems as if the land itself is telling the story.

Myth thus coalesces with autobiography; indeed, Native Americans employ similar techniques of storytelling in each genre. Narrators will often recount their own life stories using mythological tales and songs, creating a legend about themselves whose form is reminiscent of that of familiar collective myths.

Myths will often be told on particular occasions when they have a special meaning for an individual. For example, when a Tlingit man who

An 1880s poster advertising the "Wild West Fair" in New York's Madison Square Garden. Staged by the hunter-turned-entrepreneur William F. ("Buffalo Bill") Cody, this pageant presented a highly romanticized picture of life on the Plains. Cody respected Indian values, and persuaded the Lakota chief Sitting Bull to appear, but his show helped to form a patronizing and trivialized image of Indian life that prevailed for almost a hundred years.

134

The Impact of Christianity

From the beginning of the white presence in the Americas, the theft of Indian lands was matched by a systematic destruction of their religion. There were strong incentives for Indians to convert to Christianity in order to secure trade concessions or protection from traditional enemies.

In many respects, Christianity was wholly unfamiliar to Native Americans. The Christian emphasis on Heaven was alien to the holistic Indian view of the universe, and the hierarchy and liturgy of organized religion counter to their notion of voluntary communion with the divine. Yet other features were more familiar. The fortitude and suffering of Catholic saints resembled that of Native hero figures, while the element of sacrifice central to the Eucharist found an echo in the self-sacrifice of the vision quest and the Sun Dance.

While indigenous religious traditions assimilated many elements of the white settlers' religion, such tolerance and openness were not displayed by the Christian Church. Ecclesiastical and government agencies forced Indians to destroy their masks and other sacred objects and enacted hostile legislation. In 1883 the US Code of Religious Offences banned many important Native rites, while around the same time Canada outlawed the vital Northwest Coast potlatch ceremony.

A Pueblo Indian hide painting of the Madonna (1675) gives evidence of early influence by Spanish missionaries.

had served overseas during the Second World War finally returned home, his mother sang him a song about the adventures of Kaakha'achgook, a famous ancestor of the Tlingit. Despite bad omens warning him to stay at home, Kaakha'achgook had been compelled to go hunting sea mammals in order to feed his wives. He was blown off course and marooned for a long time on a small island, where he devised ingenious ways of staying alive. Eventually, he found his way home, but had difficulty coming to terms with all the changes that had taken place during his absence. In performing this song, the modern soldier's mother was acknowledging the hardships that he had endured, as well as suggesting the problems he would face in adjusting to civilian life.

The Western Apache habitually forge a strong link between event and location by beginning and ending their myths and stories with the phrase, "It happened at such-and-such a place." Moreover, these narratives are often intended to exert a moral influence on the listener. The Apache say that they "shoot each other" with stories, as they would with arrows. Telling a story, then, can be a warning that the listener is behaving badly in some way, and if he does not change his ways, something unpleasant will happen to him. The person "shot" can resolve to "pull the arrow out" by addressing the problem.

Traditional Western Apache stories also serve as a way of transmitting ethical values to future generations. Children who are ignorant of stories relating to their homeland are said to be "losing the land" and are expected to encounter difficulties in later life. In educating through storytelling, Apache teachers always ensure that they relate the action and location of the story to the child's personal situation.

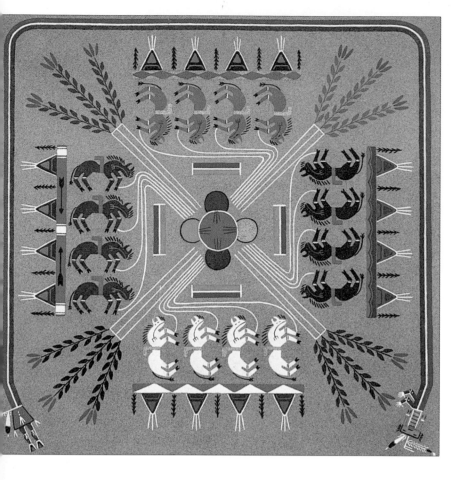

A sandpainting entitled *Homes of the Buffalo People* (1979), by the Navajo artist Herbert Ben, Sr. Sandpainting is just one of many Native art forms that continue to thrive in North America.

From Myth to Literature

Traditional Native arts such as storytelling and dancing are often now recast in modern idioms – for example, the theatre. In this way, they both reach a wide audience and take on a pan-Indian identity. At the same time, many writers aim to bridge the gap between Native and white cultures. Much Native poetry tries to preserve the rhythms of Native languages even when written in English. This is a difficult endeavour, as the oral tradition does not easily lend itself to translation into the written word. A Washo story tells how, in 1910, a man who later became a shaman was cured by his uncle, who pulled a piece of printed matter out of his patient's head and told him that he had fallen ill from studying books, which belonged to the white people's world. By contrast, the contemporary Native poet Duane Niatum writes that a Native American writer "must train himself to become sensitive to the many facets of the English language, with the same devotion that a shaman had for his healing songs a thousand years ago".

Since the 1960s, the modern Native American experience has been the subject of several notable novels, such as *House Made of Dawn* (N. Scott Momaday), which won the Pulitzer Prize for Fiction in 1969, *Ceremony* (Leslie Marmon Silko) and *The Death of Jim Lonely* (James Welch). A situation of conflict is immediately established in the fact that the central characters are (like their authors) of mixed blood and are torn between reservation and city life. However, the conflict is ultimately resolved when the characters restore their relationship with the land and its tribal traditions. Similarly, for the authors the very act of writing is a cathartic reaffirmation of their Native roots.

The telling of stories and myths is integral to the healing process. The message of much Indian literature is that white people are out of sympathy with the land because they are driven to conquer and dominate it, whereas the Native approach is to listen to what the land has to say and discover a way of living in harmony with it. In a disorienting world, such literature aims to make people whole again by reference to ancient patterns of order and meaning that are enshrined in the oral tradition of storytelling.

Red and White Roads

The way in which Native artists and writers reflect on their own situation contrasts dramatically with the portrayal of Native Americans by white society. The brutal racism of the "Wild West", reinforced by countless films, stereotyped Indians as cruel barbarians. Another convention, epitomized by James Fenimore Cooper's *The Last of the Mohicans* (1826), cast the Indian as a doomed romantic figure. This partially represented the truth: at that time many Indian communities were beset by depression, alcoholism and violence, their sacred bundles confiscated by missionaries and their ancestors' skeletons stolen and publicly displayed in museums. Yet even many sympathetic early images of Native Americans reflected white prejudice and misconception: merely because the Inuit had never resisted white domination, they were shown as happy and naïve.

A positive evaluation of Native American culture by large sections of white society only began with the "counterculture" of the 1960s, a period that also witnessed the rise of Indian militancy. John G. Niehardt's book *Black Elk Speaks*, ignored since its publication in 1932, came to be regarded as the great religious classic of twentieth-century North America. Similarly, a series of books by Carlos Castañeda, purportedly documenting his apprenticeship to a Yaquí shaman, Don Juan, and his subsequent mystical experiences, stimulated huge interest in Native spirituality. Castañeda's works became best-sellers on both sides of the Atlantic. Young people, in particular, came to think of Native North Americans as possessing a spirituality that their own society had lost, and hoped to learn from their traditional beliefs. However, the wholesale appropriation of Native forms of worship by some whites was denounced by many in the Indian community as a new form of imperialism.

At the same time as white interest in Indian religions was growing, Indians themselves formed pressure groups to lobby for a restitution of their rights. One result of this movement was the passing, in 1990, of an Act of Congress that finally required all government-sponsored institutions to return Native American ancestral remains for proper burial and sacred objects for correct devotional use.

Perhaps the greatest lesson that Native American culture can teach contemporary society concerns the environment. In 1992 Chief Oren Lyons of the Houdenosaunee, or Iroquois, pointed out that, although the Iroquois Confederacy had helped to draft the constitution of the United States in the 1780s, the new country had unwisely chosen not to adopt Indian provisions for safeguarding the earth for future generations.

A powwow at Bismarck in North Dakota. These secular gatherings are important occasions for Native Americans publicly to reaffirm pride in their cultural identity.

Glossary

adobe Building material made of earth mixed with straw and baked in the sun; constructed of adobe.

Algonquian A family of languages spoken in the Northeast and on the Plains; also used to refer to any people speaking an Algonquian language, such as the Cree, the Micmac and the Cheyenne. Also spelled Algonkian.

Anasazi An ancient culture of the Southwest that flourished *c.*AD700–1300; of or pertaining to this culture.

Athabascan A family of languages spoken in the Subarctic and the. Southwest; also used of any people speaking an Athabascan language, such as the Beaver and the Navajo. Also spelled Athapascan and Athapaskan.

buffalo In this book, "buffalo" always refers to the North American buffalo, or bison.

butte A flat-topped hill, geologically similar to a mesa but covering a smaller area.

caribou A large species of ungulate inhabiting the northern tundra. The domesticated form of the animal is known as reindeer.

clan A group comprised of a number of related families from several households; the most important unit of social organization among many Native American peoples, notably on the Northwest Coast.

crest An image of a creature, typically a blend of the animal, human and supernatural, used as a heraldic device by clans and families, who trace their origins and even recent histories back to their encounter with such beings.

earthdiver A being which, in one common type of Native creation myth, dives to the bottom of the primeval waters to retrieve soil, from which the first dry land is then formed.

Iroquoian A family of languages spoken in the Northeast; also used to refer to any people speaking an Iroquoian language, such as the Iroquois and the Huron.

Iroquois The collective name given to several Iroquoian-speaking peoples of the northeastern United States and southeastern Canada. Specifically, it refers to six Iroquois peoples who formed an alliance known as the Iroquois League or the Six Nations (the Cayuga, Mohawk, Oneida, Onondaga, Seneca and Tuscarora).

kachina Among the Hopi and other Pueblo peoples, a kachina is a benevolent ancestral spirit or deity. Kachinas participate in important festivals in the form of masked impersonators in dance rituals.

kiva A partly subterranean chamber used for important rituals and ceremonies by the Hopi and other Pueblo peoples. The term is also used for similar structures characteristic of the ancient cultures of the region, such as the Anasazi.

longhouse A type of rectangular dwelling that is home to several families. Longhouses were formerly characteristic of the Iroquois and other peoples of the Northeast.

medicine bundle A bundle of holy objects that are believed to possess special significance or to be a source of "medicine" (spirit power) for an individual. It is similar to a sacred bundle.

mesa A flat-topped elevated region, similar to a plateau but covering a smaller area.

potlatch A ceremony, common on the Northwest Coast, in which an individual affirms his prestige or rank by giving away or even destroying material possessions; important transactions are also witnessed at potlatches.

precontact Of or pertaining to the period before the first contact between Europeans and Native people.

prehistoric Of or pertaining to the time before written historical records, i.e. any period for which knowledge is based mainly on oral tradition and archaeology. In Native North American terms, this may refer to any time before the arrival of Europeans.

pueblo (Spanish: "village") 1. A traditional town or village of the Southwest constructed of adobe or stone. 2. (With capital "P") A people of whom such settlements are characteristic, such as the Hopi and the Taos.

sacred bundle A bundle of holy objects that are believed to possess special significance or to be a source of great spirit power for a tribe or group. It is similar to a medicine bundle.

sweat lodge A building in which community members are purified or ritually cleansed by sweating; it takes the form of either a wigwam-like structure or a large semi-underground lodge.

tipi A conical tent of buffalo hide or canvas. It is of Plains origin but was adopted by some other tribes owing to the ease with which it can be dismantled and transported by horse. Also spelled teepee.

tribe To anthropologists, a community that shares cultural traits and has a specific geographical location. Native North Americans apply the term broadly to entities as small as a clan, or as large as the inhabitants of an entire reservation.

wigwam A domed tent of bark or matting, formerly the characteristic dwelling of some Algonquian peoples.

Index

Page numbers in *italic* relate to illustration captions. Where there is a textual reference to the topic on the same page as the caption, italics have not been used.

Further Reading

Bierhorst, J. *The Mythology of North America,* William Morrow, New York, 1985

Billard, J. B. *The World of the American Indian,* National Geographic Society, Washington D.C., 1974

Brody, H. *Maps and Dreams,* Douglas and McIntyre, Vancouver, 1981

Brody, H. *Living Arctic,* Douglas and McIntyre, Vancouver, 1987

Brown, Dee *Bury My Heart at Wounded Knee, An Indian History of the American West,* Simon and Schuster, New York, 1981

Champagne, D. (ed.) *Native America: Portrait of the Peoples,* Visible Ink Press, Detroit, Michigan, 1994

Cove, J. J., and G. F. McDonald (eds.) *Tsimshian Narratives I: Tricksters, Shamans and Heroes,* Canadian Museum of Civilization, Mercury Series, Ottawa, 1987

Deloria, V. *God is Red, a Native View of Religion,* North American Press, Golden, Connecticut, 1992

Driver, H. E. *Indians of North America,* University of Chicago Press, Chicago, 1961

Fagan, B. *Ancient North America,* Thames and Hudson, London and New York, 1995

Gill, S. D. *Beyond the Primitive, the Religions of Nonliterate Peoples,* Prentice Hall, Englewood Cliffs, New Jersey, 1982

Hardin, T. (ed.) *Legends and Lore of the American Indians,* Barnes and Noble Inc., New York, 1993

Jonaitis, A. *From the Land of the Totem Poles,* American Museum of Natural History, New York, 1988

Josephy, A. M. *Now that the Buffalo's Gone: A Study of Today's American Indians,* University of Oklahoma Press, Norman, 1985

Josephy, A. M. *Five Hundred Nations: An Illustrated History of North American Indians,* Hutchinson, New York, 1995

Kopper, P. *The Smithsonian Book of North American Indians: Before the Coming of the Europeans,* Smithsonian Institution Press, Washington D.C., 1986

Kupferer, H. J. *Ancient Drums, Other Moccasins, Native North American Cultural Adaptation,* Prentice Hall, Englewood Cliffs, New Jersey, 1988

Maxwell, J. A. (ed.) *America's Fascinating Indian Heritage,* Reader's Digest, Pleasantville, New York, 1978

Maurer, E. M. (ed.) *Visions of the People, a Pictorial History,* Minneapolis Institute of Arts, Minneapolis, 1992

Mooney, J. *The Ghost Dance Religion and the Outbreak of 1890,* University of Nebraska Press, London, 1991

Niehardt, J. *Black Elk Speaks,* University of Nebraska Press, Lincoln, Nebraska, 1979

Sturtevant, W. C. (gen. ed.) *Handbook of North American Indians,* Smithsonian Institution Press, Washington D.C., 1981

Waldman, Carl *Atlas of the North American Indian,* Facts on File, New York, 1984

Woodhead, H. (series ed.) *The American Indians,* Time-Life Books, Richmond, Virginia, 1994

Picture Credits

Key: t top; **b** bottom; **c** centre; **l** left; **r** right

AMNH:	American Museum of Natural History
BAL:	Bridgeman Art Library
BBHC:	Buffalo Bill Historical Center, Cody, Wyoming
JBT/ECT:	John Bigelow Taylor/The Eugene and Clare Thaw Collection.
BM:	British Museum
NMAA:	National Museum of American Art
MNAI:	Museum of the North American Indian
WFA:	Werner Forman Archives

3 WFA/Portland Art Museum; **5** Frans Lanting/Zefa; **6** John Anderson Collection, Smithsonian Institution (44258); **7** WFA/Maxwell Museum of Anthropology; **8-9** The Detroit Institute of Arts, Gift of Mr and Mrs Pohrt (1988.226); **10** WFA/C. Pohrt Collection. BBHC; **11** JBT/ECT (T106); **12** Corbis/Smithsonian Institution (20003881); **14l** WFA/Maxwell Museum of Anthropology; **14r** WFA; **15l** Tony Stone Images /Richard Cooke III; **15r** Corbis/Bettman; **16** Library of Congress (LC-USZ62- 602498); **17** Philbrook Museum of Art (1951.8); **18tl** Ohio State Historical Society; **18tr** Images Colour Library; **18b** Hutchison Library; **19t** Spectrum; **19bl** WFA; **19br** Images Colour Library; **20** JBT/ECT (T177); **21** BAL/NMAA; **22** WFA/RL Anderson Collection, BBHC; **23t** WFA/Portland Art Museum; **23r** WFA/Cleveland Museum of Art; **24** WFA/Schindler Coll. NY; **25** WFA/Smithsonian Institution; **26** Wheelwright Museum of the American Indian, Santa Fe, New Mexico (P-1A-8); **27** Roland Reed/Kramer Gallery, DBP Archives; **28** Hutchison Library; **29** BAL/MNAI; **30** BAL/NMAA; **31** Peter Furst/Museum für Völkerkunde, Berlin; **32** JBT/ECT (T60); **33** Peter Furst/Priv.Coll.; **34** JBT/ECT (T86); **35** University Museum Archives, University of Pennsylvania (obj: 38736); **36** WFA/BM; **37** WFA/Smithsonian Institution; **38** WFA/Haffenreffer Museum, Brown University, Rhode Island; **40** BAL/NMAA; **41** Peter Furst/Smithsonian Institution; **42** Corbis/Library of Congress, Roland Reed (LC-USZ62- 48427); **44t** Peter Furst/Priv.Coll.; **44b** Richard Cooke III/Tony Stone Images; **44–45** Ashmolean Museum, Oxford (neg EM4); **45t** America Hurrah; **45r** Stephen Myers/AMNH (3822(2)); **46** Images Colour Library; **47** Images Colour Library; **48** Ohio State Historical Society; **49** BAL; **50** Corbis; **52** WFA/Provincial Museum of Victoria, BC; **53** Corbis; **54** BAL/Princeton Museum of Natural History; **55** WFA/AMNH; **56** JBT/ECT; **57** Stephen Myers/AMNH (3837(3)): **58** National Museum of the American Indian (2336); **60** WFA/NMAI; **62** Peter Furst Priv.Coll.; **64** WFA/Museum of Anthropology, University of BC; **65** Burke Museum (117); **66** M. Holford; **68** Peter Furst/The Detroit Institute of Arts; **69** Peter Furst/Lowie Museum of Anthropology, University of California at Berkeley; **71** M. Holford; **72** Peter Furst/Priv.Coll.; **73** WFA; **74** Corbis/Library of Congress; **75** JBT/ECT (T43); **76** Peter Furst/Priv. Coll.; **78** Peter Furst/Priv.Coll.; **79** America Hurrah; **80l** America Hurrah; **80r** Wheelwright Museum of the American Indian, Santa Fe; **81** WFA/BBHC; **82-83** JBT/ECT (T185); **84** BAL; **84** WFA; **86** WFA/Field Museum of Natural History, Chicago; **88** BAL; **89** Peter Furst/Priv.Coll.; **90** State Historical Society of North Dakota (SHSND 12004); **91** Peter Furst/Priv. Coll.; **92** Peter Furst/Priv.Coll.; **93** BAL; **94** BAL; **96** Peter Furst/Peabody Museum of Natural History, Yale University; **97** Peter Furst/Smithsonian Institution; **98** Tony Stone Images; **99** BAL; **100c** Peter Furst/Priv.Coll.; **100b** BAL; **100-101** JBT/ECT (T49); **101t** WFA/BM; **101b** State Historical Society of North Dakota (SHSND 941); **102** Robert Harding Picture Library; **103** Paul Macapia/Seattle Museum of Art (91.1.124); **104t** Robert Harding Picture Library; **104b** Robert Harding Picture Library; **105** Royal Anthropological Institute, London (RAI 2075); **106** Peter Furst/Priv.Coll.; **107** AMNH (41184); **108** Peter Furst/Priv. Coll.; **109** Ohio State Historical Society; **110** Special Collections Division of the University of Washington Libraries (NA3151); **112** WFA/Portland Art Museum; **113** Peter Furst/Priv.Coll.; **114** Library of Congress/Edward S. Curtis (LC-USZ62-101185); **115** WFA /Provincial Museum of Victoria, BC; **116** AMNH (42298); **117** Canadian Inuit Art Information Centre, Ottawa (PAN23PR7613); **118** Peter Furst/Priv.Coll.; **119** WFA/Musuem für Völkerkunde, Berlin; **120** Stephen Myers/AMNH (3847(2)); **121** Corbis/Library of Congress; **122** Smithsonian Institution (86-2842); **123** WFA/Field Museum of Natural History, Chicago; **124** Bryan & Cherry Alexander; **125** WFA/BBHC; **126** WFA/Glenbow Museum, Alberta; **127** Philbrook Museum of Art/Richard West (1949.20); **128** America Hurrah; 130 JBT/ECT (T86); **131** America Hurrah; **132l** BAL/BM; **132rc** BAL; **132rb** BAL; **133tl** M. Holford/BM; **133tr** BAL/BM; **133b** BAL; **134** BAL; **135** BAL; **136** Peter Furst/Priv. Coll.; **137** Tony Stone Images